LOVE AND COMPASSION

Exploring Their Role in Education

Teachers often speak about their love for their subject, their students, and their vocation.

As multidimensional as love is, it can be a taboo subject relative to teachers and students. In *Love and Compassion*, John P. Miller explores different forms of love, including self-love, love of others, love of beauty, and love of learning, and how they can be nurtured in an educational setting to improve teaching and learning.

Love and Compassion is both a practical and conceptual work, and will interest those involved in the study and practice of holistic and contemplative education. In addition to the different dimensions of love, Miller discusses nonviolent action and compassion and how they are crucial to the practice of teaching, and reflects on his own and his students' experiences with creating a loving environment in the classroom.

JOHN P. MILLER is a professor in the Department of Curriculum, Teaching, and Learning at the Ontario Institute for Studies in Education, University of Toronto.

JOHN P. MILLER

LOVE

AND

COMPASSION

Exploring Their Role in Education

UNIVERSITY OF TORONTO PRESS
Toronto Buffalo London

© University of Toronto Press 2018
Toronto Buffalo London
www.utorontopress.com

ISBN 978-1-4875-0331-4 (cloth)   ISBN 978-1-4875-2257-5 (paper)

Library and Archives Canada Cataloguing in Publication

Miller, John P., 1943–, author
Love and compassion : exploring their role in education / John P. Miller.

Includes bibliographical references and index.
ISBN 978-1-4875-0331-4 (cloth). ISBN 978-1-4875-2257-5 (paper)

1. Love. 2. Compassion. 3. Teaching. 4. Education. I. Title.

BF575.L8M55 2017 177'.7   C2017-905229-2

This book has been published with the help of a grant from the Federation
for the Humanities and Social Sciences, through the Awards to Scholarly
Publications Program, using funds provided by the Social Sciences and
Humanities Research Council of Canada.

University of Toronto Press acknowledges the financial assistance to its
publishing program of the Canada Council for the Arts and the Ontario Arts
Council, an agency of the Government of Ontario.

Canada Council   Conseil des Arts
for the Arts   du Canada

ONTARIO ARTS COUNCIL
CONSEIL DES ARTS DE L'ONTARIO
an Ontario government agency
un organisme du gouvernement de l'Ontario

Funded by the   Financé par le
Government   gouvernement
of Canada   du Canada

Canadä

To the loving memory of
Joy and Jean

Contents

Foreword

I've known Jack Miller for many years – at a distance, for the most part, working on various projects, all having to do with giving education a heart. I remember the first time I sat with him in Toronto, in his home that was filled with his friends. I soaked in his uncommon blend of warmth and intelligence, compassion and conviction. So I'm not surprised that he has written another inspiring book that gets to the heart of the matter: the connection between love and learning.

The book explores the many sides and kinds of love: friendship, community, self-appreciation, curiosity, the love of learning, and love for what you study. With so much love surrounding the experience of learning, as Jack describes it anyway, it's surprising that educators don't talk more about love. But, as Jack explains, love can be embarrassing to many people. They would rather keep their teaching and learning emotionally cool.

And, of course, there is the shadow of love: teachers getting involved with students and children falling in love with fields and subjects that upset their parents. How many stories are told of famous artists who had to run away from home to pursue the art they loved rather than the skill set their parents hoped would give them financial security.

Psychology needs to teach people that shadow is an inescapable and ultimately valuable part of anything. We just have to learn to process it, own it, and watch it transform into something worthwhile and sometimes beautiful.

My favourite part of this book is Jack's description of his classroom, where students have the freedom to love and explore and relate and experiment. As I read these passages, I felt I was back in college reading Abraham Maslow, who wrote in a similar style that was both substantive and light, practical and inspiring.

But there are always those who build their educational theory on anxiety, afraid that if they can't cover all subjects and train their students rigorously, those young people won't get good jobs. You don't find that anxiety in Jack Miller's approach to learning. Instead, you read about contemplation, mindfulness, and friendly interactions in the classroom.

How can anyone be successful in their work or as a person if they don't love what they do? How can a young person today sustain their love of learning, if they ever had it, in a dehumanizing environment? Only if we have Jack Miller showing us intelligently and precisely how to infuse our education with love.

This is a beautiful book. And, by the way, Jack follows a long philosophical tradition by connecting love and the beautiful. He quotes Thoreau saying that our goal is a beautiful education. Imagine our political leaders standing up asking us to support a beautiful education. Beauty, love, and pleasure are the values proclaimed over the centuries by champions of a soulful culture, notably the early Greeks, leaders of the European Renaissance, and the Transcendentalists of Concord.

I would like to see this book taken seriously as a model for an educational renaissance in which we bring soul to the classroom – depth, meaningfulness, pleasure, friendship, and love. My problem is not so much with the subjects we teach as the way we teach them. I had a client once who had a passion for accounting. Why not? He would have been fortunate to find a school where he could study numbers and tables in a loving way, seeing their beauty, and even grasping their poetic resonance. I'd call my course "The Art of Accounting" or maybe "The Beauty of Numbers."

I am proud to have been associated, if somewhat remotely, with Jack Miller over these years. I have learned much from his previous books and feel that we are comrades in a world that often just can't grasp the truly important issues, like love, friendship, and contemplation.

Finally, a word to the reader. Reading this book is itself an experience of education. Take time to consider where you are coming from. Try to get to the point where you actually feel love for Jack Miller, his students, and the creative people he cites. Befriend the ideas here. Put the central idea of this book into practice. Understand that your reading is complete only when you consider ways to transform learning through the force of love.

Thomas Moore

Acknowledgments

I am grateful to all the students I have worked with at the Ontario Institute for Studies in Education (OISE). They provided the environment and support so that this book could happen. The students are present throughout the book with their own experiences and comments. So many of their experiences, however, could not be included, yet somehow their spirit can be found here. Simply put, the students have inspired me and, now in my seventy-fourth year, I still look forward to teaching. The energy and the love that can arise in my classes keep calling me back to the classroom.

I am also appreciative of the support I received from OISE, which provided a year-long leave for me to write this book. My courses in Holistic and Contemplative Education are not in the mainstream and, since 1988, I have required students to meditate in my courses. I am grateful for the support of my institution for being able to do this work, which would not have been possible in some universities.

Some of the material used in chapters 3 and 6 is taken from *Education and the Soul*, published by SUNY Press. Some of the material in chapter 8 and the material in the appendix were published in *The Contemplative Practitioner: Meditation in Education and the Workplace*, published by University of Toronto Press, and is reprinted here with permission.

I am also grateful to the University of Toronto Press which has published several of my books. A special thank you to Douglas Hildebrand for guiding the manuscript through the review process. I am also grateful to Beth McAuley for copy editing the manuscript, and to Lisa Jemison, managing editor at the University of Toronto Press, for guiding the production process.

I am fortunate that Thomas Moore has done the foreword to this book. His work has continued to be a source of inspiration.

Finally, a big thank you to my wife, Midori, who proofread this manuscript and who is a loving presence in my life.

LOVE AND COMPASSION

Exploring Their Role in Education

1
Love: An Introduction

"Love is our true destiny."

– Thomas Merton

I teach graduate courses in holistic education and contemplative education to teachers. In one class students were making a presentation and a paper was circulated where students wrote down what they were experiencing. One person wrote, "There is a lot of love in this room." I have felt this same sense of love in many of my other classes. I just finished a course where there was a strong sense of love. One student wrote this:

> Simply put, I feel this course is about healing one another. To me, it is "home" as it has been welcoming and inviting enough to allow me to develop close and intimate relationship with many people whom I had just met. I also find this course real, authentic, and organic. It is first and foremost about us, one human being to another, about opening our hearts, reaching out and supporting one another, sharing our stories of joy and sorrow, our moments of vulnerability and allowing ourselves to feel empathy at a very deep and personal level.

In this course, The Teacher as Contemplative Practitioner, students made presentations that lasted about thirty to forty minutes; many students shared their personal journeys as well as their spiritual beliefs and practices. There was real diversity in the class in terms of religion, race, and sexual orientation. A woman from Saudi Arabia, a Muslim, wrote the passage above and talked about her faith while a young woman from China talked about Taoism in her presentation. A Christian shared her practice of daily Bible readings while a Jewish man gave a presentation on Buddhism. A person who had transitioned from being a woman to man while "they" were teaching an elementary class talked about his journey.

Many students, I believe, experienced love in this class. But what is love in an educational setting? Should it be nurtured in an era of accountability? If so, how? What are the conditions that support love in classrooms and schools? These are some of the questions that I explore in this book.

bell hooks (2000) is one of a few academics who has written extensively about love. She says that it has not been easy.

> When I talked of love with my generation, I found it made everyone nervous or scared, especially when I spoke about not feeling loved enough. On several occasions as I talked about love with friends, I was told I should consider seeing a therapist. I understood that a few friends were simply weary of my bringing up the topic of love and felt that if I saw a therapist it would give them a break. But most folks were just frightened of what might be revealed in any exploration of meaning of love in our lives. (xix)

In the world of academia that I inhabit, words like "love," "soul," and "beauty" are rarely explored. Diane Ackerman has written about how as a "society we are embarrassed by love" (cited in hooks 2000, 1). Cornel West (2008) is another academic who has not been afraid to write about love. He writes that "it is steadfast commitment to the well-being of others" (156).

Barbara Fredrickson (2014) has been studying what she calls the biology of love and how love is deeply embedded in our interactions with others. In her research she has found that love is connection. More specifically she writes, "Love is the momentary upwelling of three tightly interwoven events: first, a sharing of one or more positive emotions between you and another; second, a synchrony between your and the other person's biochemistry and behaviors; and third, a reflected motive to invest in each other's well-being that brings mutual care" (17). This experience can give rise to a sense of oneness where we feel connected to something larger than ourselves. This definition of love would help clarify what sometimes occurs in the classroom, since Fredrickson argues that love occurs within interpersonal transactions that can arise in any group setting. She writes, "Love unfolds and reverberates between and among people" (19).

Fredrickson (2014) believes that "love is the supreme emotion" since it lets us be whole human beings where we feel fully alive (11). It also allows us to "*see* another person, holistically with care, concern, and compassion" (11). My field is holistic education, with compassion as one of its central goals along with wisdom, well-being, wholeness, and sense of purpose. Fredrickson focuses on love as an emotion that arises and passes away depending on the conditions. As important as Fredrickson's research is, love can be viewed from a variety of perspectives. Love is multidimensional and exists in various forms and even exists beyond form as a universal energy: Eros.

The various forms of love explored in this book include:

- Self-love
- Personal love
- Impartial love: Compassion
- Love of learning
- Love of beauty
- Love as nonviolent action
- Presence, love as a way of being
- Eros or universal love

The rest of this chapter briefly introduces these various forms and their connection to education.

Self-Love

bell hooks (2000) writes, "It is no easy task to be self-loving" (54). Instead, it is easier to doubt ourselves. Our parents and schooling may have contributed to our self-doubt by creating expectations that we were supposed to meet. These expectations can have the effect of learning not to trust our own experience; instead, we look to others to validate what is happening to us. These individuals can include an older sibling, teachers, or our peers, and we can internalize feelings of self-doubt from things they say or the non-verbal messages that we perceive. This internalization has been called the inner critic.

Self-love involves learning to trust our own organism, that is, our body, our intuitions, and our experience. Self-love involves making friends with ourselves. The chapter on self-love will discuss ways that we can begin to re-inhabit our bodies and our whole being. Mindfulness and meditation practices are helpful. This work is not about building superficial self-esteem. It is about seeing ourselves as part of nature and the universe. Nature can be used as a guide to self-acceptance.

Personal Love

Personal love involves both romantic love as well other forms such as friend-ship. Romantic love in our culture has been trivialized through soap operas and Harlequin romances, or is the target of cynicism. Yet romantic love can teach us a great deal. When we fall in love, we see the angelic nature of the beloved. Some say this is a romantic illusion, but perhaps we see the other's true nature. Through love the soul touches the eternal, the divine. Still roman-tic love is more than falling in love; Linda Carroll (2014) has described five stages of love that are a helpful guide to committed relationships.

We can also have strong connections to others that are not romantic. The Japanese use the term *en* to describe powerful connection to others; it is a mysterious connection between two individuals, although it is also possible to have *en* with a group, work, or even a place. We experience *en* when we feel a strong connection to someone and when we feel the need to do some kind of work with that individual. An example of *en* is the relationship between Bill Thetford and Helen Schucman. Thetford was the head of the psychology department at the Columbia Medical School where Helen, a psychologist, also worked. Helen started to have visions that eventually led her to write *A Course in Miracles*. Not being religious, Helen had difficulty in dealing with her visions and the material that was coming through her. Bill got a very small room where they could meet and he could write down the material that was coming through Helen. This went on for seven years till the three volumes of the *Course* were completed. It is clear that the *Course* could never have been completed without this relationship. There are many other examples of *en* – Emerson and Thoreau and Helen Keller and Annie Sullivan are two others.

Finally, there is friendship. Ralph Waldo Emerson ([1940] 1968) wrote that "the essence of friendship is entireness, a total magnanimity and trust" (236). For most of us there are not many friendships of this nature. The ones that we have are to be treasured. People talk about how they can pick up a conversation with a friend that they have not seen in years. Friend-ship, then, can have a timeless quality.

These various forms of personal connections can be explored through literature. Novels, plays, and stories allow students to reflect on what love and friendship mean in their own lives.

Impartial Love: Compassion

Through wisdom and lovingkindness we can begin to see the angelic nature not only in our beloved but in all beings. We make the effort to connect to this inner core of goodness and decency in others. When giving his talks, the Dalai Lama looks out at his audience and sees beings who desire happiness and do not want to suffer. This witnessing leads naturally to compassion for others. Parents suffer with the agonies of their children as they grow and can thus feel compassion for all parents and their children. Compassion can extend to all living things and, in the last decades, there has been much more awareness of animals and greater efforts to avoid harming them. The Vietnamese monk Thich Nhat Hanh (2016) has written about compassion:

> Nothing exists by itself alone. We all belong to each other; we cannot cut reality into pieces. My happiness is your happiness; my suffering is your suffering. We heal and transform together. Every side is "our side"; there is no evil side, no enemy. (82)

Karen Armstrong (2010) has written extensively about compassion and how it is central to all faiths and spiritual traditions. She has also offered guidelines to living a compassionate life. There are now cities and schools that have taken on compassion as a central tenet.

Love of Learning

Curiosity and wanting to learn about the world are natural human traits. We see this in young children as they explore their surroundings. We can have the experience of being consumed about a particular interest and wanting to read and learn more. Susan Engel (2015), in her book *The Hungry Mind*, discusses how we can foster children's curiosity. There are two basic forms of curiosity: exploratory and directed. With the latter we can have the experience of being consumed about a particular interest and wanting to read and learn more. The history of science is filled with examples of how curiosity led individuals to devote their lives to inquiry and investigation. There is no better example than Einstein who searched for the unified theory of the universe. Einstein wrote, "It is in fact nothing short of a miracle that the modern methods of instruction have not yet entirely strangled the holy curious of inquiry" (cited in Howe 2003, 134). With the present-day emphasis on standardized testing, I do not believe Einstein would change his view about most schooling today. Indeed, it is time to honour "the holy curious of inquiry" in the student. Through this honouring, it is possible to instil a lifelong love of learning in the student.

Love of Beauty

Plato through Socrates in the *Symposium* argues that love of beauty is one of the highest forms of love. We do not hear much about beauty in discussions today about education. Waldorf education is the exception, with its strong focus on the aesthetic and the arts. Waldorf classrooms usually have beautiful drawings on the blackboard done by the teacher, and the students' books often contain amazing drawings that they have done.

Just as curiosity motivates the scientist, love of beauty can inspire the artist. Hanh (2016) and others have shown how we can see beauty in the simple aspects of nature, for example, the movement of clouds, the rushing waters of a stream, and the infinite variety of colours found in flowers. Nature, then, can inspire our love of beauty in the natural world. Thoreau wrote about "Beautiful Knowledge," which he sought through nature. Thoreau wrote:

> May I dare as I have never done. May I purify myself anew as with fire and water, soul and body. May my melody not be wanting to the season. May I gird myself to be a *hunter of the beautifu*, that nought escape me. May I attain to a youth never attained. I am eager to report the glory of the universe: may I be worthy to do it; to have got through regarding human values, so as not to be distracted from regarding divine values. (Cited in Alcott 1872, 263–4; emphasis mine)

Love of earth and its natural beauty can be a powerful motivator to prevent environmental degradation. This is "Beautiful Knowledge," which will be discussed in the sixth chapter.

Love as Nonviolent Action

Mahatma Gandhi and Martin Luther King Jr. saw love as a powerful social force through nonviolent action. Gandhi believed that "nonviolence is the law of our species" and employed it to help India become an independent country. King saw "love as the supreme unifying principle of life" that "stands at the center of nonviolence" and that was central to the civil rights movement in the late 1950s and 1960s. Nonviolence has a long history, which Peter Ackerman and Jack Duvall (2000) describe in their book *A Force More Powerful: A Century of Nonviolent Conflict*. Examples of nonviolence include Danish citizens refusing to cooperate with the Nazis in 1944, which brought life in the cities to a standstill. Another example is when Salvadoran students, doctors, and merchants organized a civic strike in 1944, which led to the overthrow of the dictator that forced him into exile.

Our culture seems addicted to violence. Violent behaviour is constantly shown on the news, in the movies, and on television. Given this environment, nonviolence is a challenging concept and even a more challenging way of living. Education provides a forum where nonviolence can be explored, and various approaches will be discussed in chapter 7.

Love as Presence

Avraham Cohen (2015) writes, "I believe that presence is equivalent to love. Giving full presence to another is, I believe, the greatest gift a person can offer" (37). When we experience the presence of another person, we can feel nourished and whole. We know that we have been heard not just in the head but by a whole being. Zen teacher Ellen Birx (2014) writes about the healing power of presence, "When you are fully present with others, they can feel it. It speaks to their hearts. There is a loving quality to presence. It connects and unites us. Loving presence heals and brings wholeness and vitality to life" (108). For Birx, presence is a "boundless field … without fences marring its natural beauty or defining its edges" (108). At this level love becomes a way of being in the world. We approach each day with reverence and respect.

Presence is central to teaching. When students sense our presence, they too can feel respected and honoured. Being present in a classroom of thirty-five students is not easy but, if we have this intention, students will recognize our effort. Presence and its role in teaching will be discussed in chapter 8.

Eros

In the ancient world, Eros's function as a god was to bring harmony to the universe. To Emerson, "Eros is a divine energy … and represents the essential cosmic force, the glue that holds the universe and humanity together" (cited in Gougeon 2007, 7). Dante also saw love as a divine energy that animates the universe and he concludes *The Divine Comedy* with the famous line that it is "Love that moves the Sun and the other stars" (2003, 894).

In chapter 9 I explore different forms of Eros. Near Death Experiences (NDEs) are one form; Jeffrey Long (2010), a physician, has conducted a major study on NDEs, including interviewing 1,300 subjects whose experiences showed common themes across different cultures. One of these themes is a powerful experience of unconditional love.

Scientists such as Einstein have written about the experience of a deep harmony in the universe. When he listened to the music of Mozart and Bach he felt this harmony. Mathematicians in their work have also experienced a deep order and harmony.

Closing Note

Love is multidimensional and manifests in many different forms. Bringing awareness of these various forms can enrich teaching and learning immeasurably. Two very different people – Thomas Merton, the Catholic contemplative, and bell hooks, the African American scholar – have both stated that "love is our destiny." I share that belief and, if it is our destiny, then we need to explore how we include love more fully in teaching and learning.

2

Self-Love

"Trust thyself: every heart vibrates to that iron string."

– Ralph Waldo Emerson

The Dalai Lama has commented on how people in North America suffer more from self-doubt than people in his country, Tibet. On my first trip to Japan in 1994 I found adolescents there not experiencing the self-consciousness that I could see in North American teenagers. Kenneth Leong (2001) goes even further when he writes, "Self-loathing is a much wider problem than is commonly recognized. The fact is that very few of us can really accept ourselves as we are" (125). Evidence for this self-hatred for young people includes self-cutting, eating disorders, and suicide. For adults, self-doubt can come from negative messages from our parents that we internalized and the guilt that can arise in daily life. For example, Leong observes himself and how he gets upset with himself over small things that can end in forms of self-loathing. He sees himself yelling at his children because they do not perform as he expects them to. After yelling at them, he inevitably feels bad and rebukes himself. Leong suggests we need to be more gentle and creative in our lives. Creative people see challenging situations as opportunities for spiritual growth rather than seeing them as threats. "Love, creativity, and gentleness are closely linked. People who are creative and open to life are more able to love others and themselves" (214). Being gentle with ourselves is critical to self-love.

bell hooks (2000) writes that "self-acceptance is hard for many of us" (56). To love others, we need to begin by making friends with ourselves. This involves bringing non-judgmental awareness to our behaviour. We learn to watch ourselves with openness and compassion. If I do get angry at my children, rather than immediately condemning myself, I can pause and stay in touch with my body. Just staying in the body for a moment can usually help prevent us from immediately judging ourselves.

This chapter will explore various ways to make friends with ourselves. We start with Moh Hardin's (2011) method of "being your own best friend."

Being Your Own Best Friend

Hardin's (2011) approach is based on Buddhism and the idea that within each of us is a basic goodness. Most spiritual traditions start with the idea that within us is this goodness. In some traditions, this goodness is seen as divine; for example, the Hindus identify this place as the Atman, and Jesus said the kingdom of God is within. Whatever the word we use to describe this place, it is one where we feel connected and not separate. It is a place of love. In Buddhism, it is called *Buddha nature*. Hardin writes:

> Basic goodness is a natural, clear, and uncluttered state of our being that is always at our core. It is natural in the sense that it does not have to be created or maintained in any way. It is already here. It is clear because it perceives perfectly, without any distortions, whatever is happening at this very moment, like a flawless digital video camera. It is uncluttered because it is empty of all the schemes and paranoia of the ego's story lines. (16)

Part of the process of being our own best friend is reminding ourselves that this basic goodness lies within and is always there. Spiritual practices are meant to remind us of this place within and to nourish it. Hardin (2011) describes a three-step method for being friends with ourselves.

The first step is being aware of what we feel in the moment. Hardin (2011) suggests that we bring a gentle awareness to how our body is feeling in the present moment. We can be feeling "good, bad, emotional, depressed, angry, in love, anxious, peaceful whatever it might be" (19). This initial step can be summed up as "I am here and I feel like this." Hardin suggests this gentle acceptance in the moment is also an act of courage as we face what we are actually experiencing. If there is difficulty, it does require bravery. Our culture has many enticements such as television, alcohol, and drugs to keep us from being in touch with what is happening to us.

The second step is extending kindness to yourself. Hardin (2011) says that kindness includes "acceptance, intelligence and love" (20). The love that Hardin refers to here is an "open love" that we extend to ourselves.

It allows us to experience lovingkindness. The practice of lovingkindness often starts with ourselves and gradually moves out to others. However, we often move quickly from ourselves to others without really extending that feeling of deep love and friendship to ourselves. We can even feel guilty about this step; instead, we need to relax and be with ourselves. Enjoy our own company. If there is difficulty, we can learn to live with that as well.

The third and final step is experiencing the warmth of friendship. Hardin (2011) gives the example of how when someone holds a door open for us we can feel a simple warmth of gratitude. We can feel the same warmth from experiencing the lovingkindness that we extend to ourselves. Our bodies can feel a little lighter and perhaps more energized from this process. At the same time, Hardin points out that whatever we are experiencing we need to let it go and move on. Holding on can keep us from being in the moment, which is where we need to be. Hardin writes, "The point is to keep walking" (22).

Hardin (2011) also recommends sitting meditation as part of the process of being friends with yourself. He says, "Just sit down and be" (24). In my own teaching I have asked students to meditate every day for six weeks and then reflect on their experience. One woman who had been ill wrote,

> When I meditate I concentrate on the internal organs and the sensations they feel. I practice lovingkindness to my internal organs and actually speak to them. This seems strange but effective. I ask them to forgive me for not listening earlier to their signals of exhaustion or distress ...
>
> Meditation offers a tremendous sense of release. It is my own sanctuary and anchor during times of stress. I relish the fact that I can detach during times of stress and anxiety and practice being in the moment. I can focus on my present surroundings and be mindful ...
>
> I am aware of my yin/yang or feminine/masculine side. My masculine side is flourishing because I'm allowing it the space to speak to me during meditation. This has given me more confidence. (Miller and Nozawa 2005, 182)

Meditation allowed this woman to reconnect with her body and also her masculine side.

So many of my students have had the experience of reconnecting with themselves. Here is how another person used meditation to make friends with herself:

> Through daily meditation, I have been able to take some time for myself in order to relax, regain a sense of who I am and my physical needs. I have taken

the opportunity to meditate daily for the past six weeks (and counting) in order to take into consideration the simple things that I can do for myself to help myself feel better, such as breathing properly and taking time to really enjoy little things that I experience, as opposed to moving on to the next thing without appreciating what I've just seen or felt. (Miller and Nozawa 2005, 183)

Hardin (2011) suggests that making friends with ourselves is a journey that occurs over time. It is a gradual process of awakening and connecting with our basic goodness. For Hardin it is a journey of transformation that is a "natural process that arises from basic goodness; it is a process of uncovering what we most truly are and letting it shine" (27).

Using the breath as an anchor is often helpful in this process. The Buddhist monk Ajahn Brahm (2011) writes that when we are fully with the breath it can become the "beautiful breath." This is a place of calmness and inner freedom. "It is beautiful, joyful and happy because you are free from a whole heap of suffering" (72). The beautiful breath can be a way to making friends with ourselves. We do not need anything special, it is right there all the time. Just tuning into the breath we slow down. Thoughts seem to be less troublesome. It is also helpful if we can focus on the rising and falling of the abdomen, as breathing is deeper there. If the focus is on the chest and the upper body, the breath tends to be shallower and less effective in helping us feel calm.

The breath is also a link to nature. The rhythm of breathing can be seen as similar to the rhythms of nature, for example, night and day, sun and moon, the changing seasons. Nature itself can be a guide to how we can be friends with ourselves, which will be discussed in the second part of this chapter.

David Hunt (2010), a friend and colleague, has written about friendship that starts with being a friend with yourself. He recommends using the breath as an anchor and stopping at different times during the day to take two or three breaths. He comments that, by becoming friends with your breath, "you won't find a more valuable friend" (89).

Hunt (2010) also suggests that accepting our capabilities and "foolishness" can help us in becoming friends with ourselves. Regarding our capabilities, he suggests recalling an experience where we were performing well. As much as possible, he states that we just be with that experience and then write down highlights of the experience and what it felt like. Next, focus on why you think things were working well; what were the reasons? Based on these reflections, Hunt recommends developing actions that one can pursue in daily life. Some actions that participants in his workshops came up with were "Trust Myself," "Be Patient," Take It Easy," "Be Quiet and Listen," "Stop Judging," and "Keep Smiling" (99).

Hunt (2010) uses the same method in dealing with what he calls foolish behaviour. He suggests that we remember an incident where we regretted our behaviour. Then imagine an "open minded and good hearted person" observing the situation. Next, engage in a conversation with this person about what you could learn about your behaviour. Here you can see your shortcoming as something human. It is important to accept responsibility for your behaviour and its foolish side. Finally, reflect on the behaviour and see if this is something that needs to be changed; if change is needed, then develop an action plan to improve. Hunt continually recommends a light-hearted approach to working with our imperfections. He writes, "Accepting your own imperfections is a challenging task to carry out on your own, but if you proceed gradually and gently, the results can be more than worthwhile" (105). Self-love involves acknowledging all of our behaviour. Bringing a non-judgmental awareness to what we do is an act of love that allows us to grow in becoming a whole human being.

John Makransky (2007) recommends visualizing benefactors in your life and imagine them sending love to you. These individuals can be people you know or spiritual figures that you feel connected to. One possibility is remembering someone from your childhood who was kind to you. Once you have settled on a person, just relax and feel that person's presence and their wish to send love to you.

> Seeing these wonderful people before you, gently open to their wish of love. Imagine their wish as a gentle radiance like a soft shower of healing rays. Bathe your whole body and mind in that tender radiance, all the way down to your toes and fingertips. Bask in the loving energy of that wish. (26)

After a while, Makransky suggests that you also send love to yourself using the phrase, "May this one have deepest well-being, happiness, and joy" (27). At the end of the visualization, he suggests letting go of the benefactor and just resting in a space of peace and well-being.

Nature as a Guide

Nature can also be a guide to self-love. We can look at animals and see how they are not confused about their place in nature. A dog knows that she is a dog. Emerson (2003) comments on how humans separate themselves from nature:

> These roses under my window make no reference to former roses or to better ones; they are for what they are; they exist with God to-day. There is not time to them. There is simply the rose; it is perfect in every moment of its existence. Before a leaf-bud has burst, its whole life acts; in the full-blown flower there is no more; in the leafless root there is no less. Its nature is satisfied and it satisfies nature in all moments alike. But man postpones or remembers; he does not live in the present, but with reverted eye laments the past, or, heedless of the riches that surround him, stand on tiptoe to foresee the future. He cannot be happy and strong until he too lives with nature in the present, above time. (279)

Emerson loved walking in the woods surrounding Concord, Massachusetts, where he lived. His first book, *Nature,* is a song to nature. He writes (2003), "In the presence of nature a real delight runs through the man" (184). Sometimes our experience in nature can bring us to the divine. Catherine Gildiner (2015) describes her encounter with the Welsh countryside, which she described as a "paradise" where the trees and fields made her realize that "the colour green had infinite variations. Streams meandered through the forests and were so clear you could see the forest perfectly reflected in them" (76). She writes, "Suddenly I know what the poet Gerard Manley Hopkins meant when he said, 'The world is charged with the grandeur of God.' It was the first time I had seen God as separate from organized religion" (77).

We also see the rhythm of life in nature, as one moment we are being soaked in pouring rain and the next moment we are feeling the warmth of the sun. Nature is constantly in transition. Deng Ming-Dao (1992) makes the connection between the growth of a flower and our own development: "Just as a flower goes through stages – bud, open, bloom, pollinate, wither, fruit, fall – each of us will go through obvious stages of birth and death … We change and grow. Our identities unfold and bloom" (123). Seeing change in nature can make it easier for us to accept change in our lives. Learning to accept change is part of making friends with ourselves.

Daoism asks us to use nature as a guide in approaching life. Ming-Dao (1992) writes about what we can learn from animals:

> Those who follow Tao are fond of pointing out the wisdom of animals. When they see a cat sitting motionless in the sun or a turtle who stretches her head

upward into a still pose, they say that these animals are meditating. They know how to be still and conserve their internal energy ... Meditation is the purest and most natural expression we can have. When you look at cat or a dog sitting still and admire the naturalness of their actions, think then of your own life. Don't meditate because it is part of your schedule or is demanded by your particular philosophy. Meditate because this is natural. (294)

When we go into nature, we do not judge the trees and flowers. Alan Watts (1995) writes, "What about mountain ranges? Do you criticize the valleys for being low, and praise the peaks for being high? No. You just say, 'It is great the way it is'" (27–8). Yet we so easily find ourselves critiquing ourselves and others. Rather than critiquing what another person is wearing, it is easier to see that person as part of nature and what he or she is wearing is just another expression of nature. Once I was at a meditation retreat and one of the participants had a cold and was coughing in the meditation hall. Initially I got upset because his cough was disruptive, but then I realized his cough was just part of nature and I relaxed.

Indigenous peoples also saw nature as the primary teacher. Tatanga Mani, a member of the Stoney First Nation, compares white man's education to his own:

Oh, Yes, I went to the white man's schools. I learned to read from school books, newspapers, and the Bible. But in time I found that these were not enough. Civilized people depend too much on man-made printed pages. I turn to the Great Spirit's book which is the whole of his creation. You read a big part of that book if you study nature. You know, if you take all your books, lay them out under the sun and let the snow and rain and insects work on them for a while, there will be nothing left. But the Great Spirit has provided you and me with the opportunity for study in nature's university, the forest, the rivers, the mountain, and the animals which include us. (Cited in McLuhan 1972, 106)

One example of how Indigenous peoples use nature as a guide is the circle. Consider the words of Black Elk:

Everything the Power of the World does is done in a circle.

The sky is round, and I have heard that the earth is round like a ball, and so are all the stars. The wind, in its greatest power, whirls. Birds make their nests in circles, for theirs is the same religion as ours ... The life of a [person] is a circle from childhood to childhood, and it is in everything where power moves. (Cited in Baldwin 1994, 80)

Indigenous peoples almost always met in a circle and made decisions in that circle. The tipis in which some Indigenous peoples lived and slept was another circle that they adopted in their lives.

In my classes students sit in a circle. I believe the energy can flow more freely as everyone is sitting face-to-face. Tables are also removed so that computers are not a distraction. In this setting there is opportunity for presence and community to develop.

For centuries humans separated themselves from nature and sought control and domination of nature including animals. In recent years there has been much more sensitivity and respect for animals. Even keeping animals in zoos is being questioned. Jesus often made reference to nature and one of the most famous references was when he said,

> Don't be anxious about life, about what to eat and drink or what clothes to wear. Isn't your soul more important than food and your body more important than clothes? Look at the birds in the sky. They don't plant or harvests or store grain in barns. Your father in the sky feeds them … Look at the lilies in the field. They don't labor at the spinning wheel. But I'm sure that not even Solomon in all his glory was dressed up like one of them. If that's how God clothes the field with grass that is here today but goes into the fire tomorrow, won't he clothe you even more luxuriously? You need more trust. (Cited in Moore 2016, 37)

Thomas Moore (2016), in his recent publication *Gospel: The Book of Matthew*, adds that "Jesus teaches profound and radical trust in life as a cure for anxiety" (36). Life is a journey of learning to trust our own organisms. In the West, for centuries people were viewed as being born with original sin. Seeing ourselves as part of nature can support trusting our own organism. Watts (1995) argues that nature is "something you must trust – the birds, the bees, the flowers, the mountains, the clouds – but also inside nature, human nature" (30). He adds that "nature is not completely trustworthy" and that is part of "the risk of life." Still, living with trust in ourselves and in the cosmos is the beginning of deep happiness and joy. This is what Emerson (2003) felt when he wrote, "In the woods, we return to reason and faith. There I feel that nothing can befall me in life – no disgrace, no calamity (leaving me my eyes), which nature cannot repair" (184).

Educational Applications

In making friends with ourselves, Hardin (2011), Hunt (2010), and Brahm (2011) suggest starting with the breath. The breath can be the anchor for both teachers and students as it is always there. Here are simple instructions:

> Follow the breath as it enters the nostrils, goes down the throat, into the chest and finally feeling the rise and fall of the abdomen. Just breathe naturally. You might take one deep breath at first to get the sensation of breathing but after that just let the breathing take its own course. Experience the sensations of body breathing. Rest in the body. Thoughts will come and go. Watch them and if you get caught up in a story gently return to the breath.

Breath then becomes our home where we make friends with ourselves. We see thoughts for what they are, just thoughts. There is the phrase, "We do not have to believe what we think." Through the breath we learn to sit in that place of still awareness, which is the foundation for self-love. The chapter on presence also has examples of how being mindful can help us in this process.

Makransky's (2007) exercise, cited above, where we imagine a benefactor in our life, could also be used to help students be friends with themselves. Almost everyone has someone in their life that they feel cares for them. When students imagine that person, they are better able to nurture self-love in themselves.

Finally, have students see themselves as part of nature. Indigenous peoples' writings are very helpful here in seeing how we are part of the web of life. Just like animals and plants, we have our place on the earth and in the universe. Experiences in nature can also be healing. Take the students for a silent, mindful walk in a park or a nearby conservation area. A garden on school grounds or near the school can allow students to have direct experience with nature as well.

Closing Note

Self-love is a foundation for other forms of love. Paul Ferrini (2016) writes, "Your essence is unbroken, whole, dynamic and creative. It but awaits your trust."

Society at every level does not support self-trust. Through the media, schooling, and parenting, we learn to look outward for validation. This process is ultimately one of alienation. Spiritual practice can remind us that our essence is "unbroken, whole, dynamic and creative." Quieting down and using the breath as an anchor is one way to help reach that essence. Of course, there are others, including yoga, qigong, tai chi, and various contemplative practices. Our essence is love. The more we experience that essence, the more we can love others as we realize a life of wisdom and compassion.

3

Personal Love

"The one guardian of life is love, but to be loved you must love."

– Marsilio Ficino

I met my wife, Midori, when she translated for me when I went to Japan to conduct workshops on holistic education. Even though I could not understand what she was saying, I felt such a strong connection that it was as if we were speaking with one voice. At the end of our time working together she hugged me and something inside me broke. Love can be a force that takes over our lives. Jacob Needleman (1996) has written, "We think we can play with love, but we are mistaken. Love plays with us. It is far more powerful than we are" (18). Moore (1992) has also written that the experience can be a violent one where our world is upset and a "divine madness" takes over for a time. I have been married now to Midori for sixteen years and, although our love has developed and matured, I still treasure the memory of our first encounter.

Romantic love is one of the forms of personal love that is explored in this chapter. Other forms include friendship and what the Japanese call *en*, where we feel deep and mysterious connection with another person. Whatever the form, personal love is usually our most direct experience of love.

Love and Soul

One way of looking at romantic love is through the soul. Thomas Moore (1992), who has written several books on the soul, writes, "It may be useful to consider love less as an aspect of relationship and more as an event of the soul" (117). This was the way the ancients looked at love. From the perspective of soul, we turn to questions such as: "Does it [love] bring broader vision? Does it initiate the soul in some way? Does it carry the lover away from earth to an awareness of divine things?" (118)

Moore (1992) makes the connection between romantic love and soul and sees the two as intimately connected. He writes that "soul is not a thing but a quality or a dimension of experiencing life and ourselves. It has to do with depth, value relatedness, heart, and personal substance" (6). It is the deepest part of ourselves that we experience in many ways.

Moore (1992) cites the work of the Neo-Platonist Ficino who argued that "human love is the desire for union with a beautiful object to make eternity available to mortal life" (118). Love involves the desire for the beautiful and the eternal. This powerful force does not always work out in terms of a human relationship, yet it is primary to the deepening of the soul. Novalis, the Romantic German poet, put it this way: "love was not made for this world" (cited in Moore 1992, 118).

When we fall in love we develop an overwhelming feeling for another person. The feeling is so strong that we surrender ourselves to something greater than ourselves. In short, the ego gives up the attempt to control what is happening. Moore (1992) suggests that this loss of control "may be highly nutritious for the soul" (137). Moore claims that "love releases us into the realm of divine imagination, where the soul is expanded and reminded of its unearthly cravings and needs." He then goes on to state something that is very important: "Love allows a person to see the true angelic nature of another person, the halo, the aureole of divinity" (122).

Octavio Paz (1993) is another person who connects love and the soul. He argues that both love and soul have diminished in our materialistic culture:

> The eclipse of the soul has engendered a doubt ... about what a person really is ... A human being, having ceased to be the image and likeness of divinity, now also ceases to be a product of natural evolution and enters the category of industrial production: it is something manufactured ... So the expropriation of eroticism and love by the power of money is only one aspect of the twilight of love, the other is the vanishing of love's constitutive element – the person. The two evils complement each other and open up the perspective of a possible future of our society: technological barbarism. (204–5)

Love also has a shadow side which is recognition of inevitability of separation and death. Hegel stated, "Lovers can separate from each other only to the degree that they are mortal or when they reflect on the possibility of dying" (cited in Paz 1993, 177). Death and separation make any love poignant as the lovers realize that the physical nature of the love cannot be permanent.

Allan Bloom (1993) argues that one of the best examples of an erotic ideal is found in the story of Marcella in *Don Quixote* by Miguel de Cervantes. Marcella is a beautiful woman who, because of her beauty and her lack of response to her many suitors' overtures, is despised by men. When Don Quixote meets her and inquires about her behaviour, she states that nature made her beautiful while making all of her suitors less attractive. She suggests that they should be satisfied with contemplating her beauty rather than possessing her. Bloom comments, "Marcella's speech is perfect Socrates, Plato, and Aristotle in their erotic, cosmological, and theological teachings" (501). Like Moore and Paz, Bloom connects love and soul. This longing for the beautiful and the eternal in its most active form is "Eros, and Eros is the backbone of the soul" (544). Bloom then concludes: "Man's divination of perfect love or perfect justice is most of all what proves he has a soul" (544).

Adolescence is a time which often brings the first experience of falling in love. Yet this powerful experience is hardly touched in the school curriculum, with sometimes disastrous results as young people confront these soul-rending experiences without any preparation or guidance. The broad range of public opinion about how best to educate young people about responsible behaviour in their sexual relationships makes this a controversial topic. However, I believe that there is a way that the various conceptions of love and its relationship to soul could be discussed in the secondary school and at the university level. Works such as Plato's *Symposium* and de Cervantes's *Don Quixote* could be discussed. The student could begin to see his or her own intense personal experience from a broader and more insightful perspective. The uncharted world of their strong emotions could find place names and a road map through discussion of literature and philosophy.

Antonio T. de Nicolás (1989) does just this in a philosophy course that he teaches at the university level. One of the activities that he uses is for the students to read and re-enact Plato's *Symposium*. Through this experience and others, de Nicolás argues that students learn to imagine in a genuinely creative manner.

Sean Steel (2014), who teaches in a secondary school in Calgary, Alberta, uses Shakespeare's *Romeo and Juliet* to explore romantic love. In the play, Friar Lawrence tries to offer philosophy to soothe Romeo's passion. Romeo rejects the Friar's offerings. Steel comments, "Here, Romeo speaks the truth that all schoolteachers must face in dealing with their young students; namely that books and learning and school are ordinarily experienced by young souls not as source of love, but rather as a movement away from the lovable" (65). Romeo's intense passion is something that many adolescents can understand. Steel believes that the play explores issues around romantic love that students in high school can relate to and provides a rich forum for exploration and discussion.

The teacher can connect love to compassion. Love focuses on one person, while compassion is a more universal sentiment that is not exclusive to one person. The student can begin to see that the halo he or she sees in the beloved is inherent in every human. Through the experience of falling in love, we experience the wonder and mystery that is part of the sacredness of life; through compassion we can see the mystery and sacredness in all living things. The saint, sage, or mystic is literally one who has fallen in love with creation. The mystic is not just in love with one person but is intimate with all things.

Emerson ([1940] 1968) wrote about this expansion in his essay on Love, "In the procession of the soul from within outward, it enlarges its circles ever, like the pebble thrown into the pond, or the light proceeding from an orb ... Thus even love, which is the deification of persons, must become more impersonal every day" (218). The outcome of this expansion for Emerson is "virtue and wisdom" (220).

Romantic Love

Linda Carroll (2014) believes that "learning to love well is the crowning achievement of life" (17). She cites recent research that "love alters the pathways of the brain, strengthens the immune system, and contributes to healthy heart and organ functions" (17). She believes love is the "key" to the future of humanity. Carroll has studied the various stages that people experience in long-term relationships.

Romantic love is the first stage in a long-term relationship. Carroll (2014) calls this stage "the merge." It is a time when "life is infused with magic and fresh meaning" (7). Boundaries seem to disappear. Like Moore, Carroll believes there is "sacredness in this first stage; it is not simply an illusion" (8). Tennov (1979) describes this stage as characterized by

- feelings of ecstasy in the presence of the loved one
- deep mood swings
- overestimation of the good qualities of the beloved and minimization of the negative.

Carroll (2014) cites John Keats's (1958) letter to his wife, Fanny Brawne, as an example of this first stage:

> I cannot exist without you. I am forgetful of everything but seeing you again. My Life seems to stop there; I see no further. You have absorb'd me. I have a sensation at the present moment as though I was dissolving ... Love is my religion. I could die for that; I could die for you. My Creed is Love and you are its only tenet. You have ravish'd me away by a Power I cannot resist. (390)

Still this period does not last forever. The world and its demands reassert themselves and bring us back to earth. Carroll's (2014) next stage is doubt and denial. The first stage ends when some behaviours of our partner begin to annoy us. We can also seek time alone or simply want to see old friends. These feelings come and go as there is still the desire to re-experience the wonder of the merge. Carroll writes that this can be the silent stage as the person experiences these first feelings of doubt. Carroll suggests that our bodies begin to feel different in this stage. Rather than feeling a glow, our doubts can lead to stress hormones that makes us want to "fight, flee or freeze" (21). Growth comes from being aware of these feelings and realizing that they can arise after the romance fades. Instead of fleeing, the person can commit to working through difficulty. If a relationship is to move forward, each person must recognize the other has distinct needs that are different. Other skills that Carroll feel are important to developing whole-hearted loving include listening without barriers, learning to collaborate, and self-care.

The third stage is disillusionment. At this stage the conflict intensifies between wanting to stay in the relationship and the desire to break free. Carroll (2014) writes, "It's quite a high-wire act, to learn to simultaneously love oneself, love another, and cultivate the space between the two" (56). As difficulty arises in the relationship, there can be the tendency to listen to the inner critic. At this stage, Carroll stresses the importance of self-love discussed in the previous chapter. Self-care is essential to navigating this most difficult of the five stages.

Decision is the fourth stage. Here the person needs to address the question of whether to stay and work towards a fulfilling relationship or to withdraw. Withdrawal can mean both leaving and staying but remaining conflicted or unengaged. Carroll (2014) stresses moving slowly through this stage and not acting on impulse. She begins the chapter on this stage with a quote from Rilke, "Live the questions now. Perhaps then, someday far in the future, you will gradually without even noticing it, live your way into the answer" (77). This is a stage of reflection as we examine our past patterns and personal history as well as the patterns and issues in the relationship. Carroll suggests it may even be helpful for couples to separate for a time. Ideally this should be done with clear expectations and the help of a third person.

The final stage is wholehearted loving. The stage is both similar to and profoundly different from the first stage. Here the person has a "deep knowledge that I'm enough and can extend myself to you from a grounded place rather than the belief that I cannot live without my partner" (Carroll 2014, 172). Here there is a clear sense of boundaries. In short, we engage the relationship from a place of strength as well as with an awareness of our imperfections. Carroll (2014) references the work of Brené Brown and writes that you can feel worthy and also let "yourself be seen in the deepest part of your vulnerability" (172). Generosity usually arises here as well. Simple acts like making tea for our partner can nourish a relationship. However, as we learn to care for our partner, our wholeheartedness extends to others. Carroll makes reference to the impartial love of Buddhism, which is discussed in the next chapter, as love extended to "all sentient beings," including animals. We respond to others "with compassion, prayer, or practical action, because this is what it means to live a wholehearted life" (176).

Carroll (2014) identifies the barriers to wholehearted love. They include codependence, a closed heart, and half-hearted love. She then suggests ways of nurturing a relationship, including humour, doing new things, and playfulness. Most helpful are the Six C's – choice, commitment, celebration, compassion, co-creation, and courage. *Choice* is based again on the principle that I take responsibility for my life, which begins with feeling well and whole. Decisions made from a place of wellness do not lead to codependence. *Commitment* involves standing with our partner through the ups and downs. It also means commitment to doing the inner work that helps make a relationship flourish. *Celebration* means that joy is shared in the relationship. The couple looks for ways to cultivate well-being and happiness. This means happiness that is shared and that the well-being of each person is honoured. The relationship needs to support each person's journey and life's work. *Compassion* means that "we can forgive ourselves and forgive our partner, again and again" (195). We also experience the suffering of our partner as our own. *Co-creation* happens when the couple's bond actually builds something new that would not have happened if they were not together. This may be something material like working together or something more spiritual and invisible, which radiates out from their relationship. Finally, *courage* means being able to look clearly at each other with "awareness, honesty, and love" (196). This means not letting things slide if we feel something needs to be addressed in the relationship.

I believe Carroll's (2014) work provides a valuable map that adolescents could examine. They could apply it to love in novels and literature. Most importantly, they could use it to reflect on their own experience as love enters their own lives. Carroll's map at the very least shows the complexities and challenges of love.

En

One of the first concepts that I learned about when I went to Japan was *en*. *En* is the mysterious and deep connection between two persons. It is not necessarily romantic, but it can mean a long-term relationship that can centre on some special work or project. Two people come together to do something that would not have been possible if each individual had been working on their own. We can have *en* not only with a person but with a place. For example, we may go to a country and feel a strong connection to the place and people. *En* with a person can also be a challenging relationship. Indigenous peoples speak of "thunder beings" that come into our lives and challenge us. Dhyani Ywahoo (1987) writes, "The one who disagrees with you is serving a sacred purpose in showing you the limitation of form. Such a person may be a 'contrary,' a 'thunder being,' one who inspires deeper understanding" (124). Although not pleasant, the experience working with a thunder being can be a source of personal and spiritual growth.

One example of two people where the *en* was very strong was the relationship between Helen Keller and Anne Sullivan Macy. Anne, better known as Annie Sullivan, was hired in 1886 to teach Helen, who was blind and deaf; however, the two became lifelong companions till Anne's death in 1936. Their relationship was a complex one that changed over the years. Initially Helen's teacher, Anne, who was also disabled by partial blindness, in later years came to depend on Helen for both emotional and financial support. Kim Nielsen, who has written two biographies of Helen, has also written the story of Anne, entitled *Beyond the Miracle Worker: The Remarkable Life of Anne Sullivan Macy and Her Extraordinary Friendship with Helen Keller* (2009).

Helen and Anne were rarely apart. Once when they were separated for four days, Helen wrote, "I miss her greatly. Her departure made a great gap in my life. Love is our very life, and Teacher seems part of myself" (cited in Nielsen 2009, 144). When Anne was Helen's teacher, she used holistic approaches to learning. She read whole sentences and phrases to Helen even before she understood them and thus taught her idiomatic English. Anne also believed in the value of nature in learning, as children need "out-of-door lessons – lessons about living things … things they love and are curious about" (143). Over time the relationship changed from that of teacher–student to one of friendship. In addition to being partially blind, Anne suffered a life of depression and chronic pain and relied on Helen's friendship and support. Nielsen (2009) writes, "Their deep friendship, and Macy's willingness to allow herself to be dependent on Keller, gave meaning to Macy's life" (x). The relationship between these two women has inspired millions of people, not only those with disabilities but those who see the courage and power of their friendship. Anne saw "experimenting as central to life and growth and said there was no other way of getting knowledge" (x). In a letter to Helen in 1916, she wrote, "We have only to keep a stiff upper lip and do our damnedest" (x).

A second example of *en* is the relationship between Helen Schucman and Bill Thetford. Both were psychologists at Columbia Medical School. In 1965 Helen, who was an atheist, started to hear an inner voice that was dictating words to her. She was troubled by this and told Bill, who was the head of the psychology department. She did not want to listen to this inner voice; however, Bill convinced her to take notes on what she was hearing. Bill's office was in a corner in the department where they would do this work. Over the next seven and a half years she filled more than 100 shorthand notebooks, which Bill then typed. The material sat around for a few years as Helen and Bill were not sure what to do with it. With help of others, it was eventually published by the Foundation for Inner Peace as *A Course in Miracles* in 1975, and has since been translated into twenty-two languages. The *Course* is about love and forgiveness. Whatever one may think of the *Course*, the story of two people coming together to do this work is a good example of *en*. Clearly, the *Course* would have not happened if they had not done so.

En between two people does not have to be at the level of the Keller–Macy relationship. However, from the soul's perspective, if one recognizes *en* with another person, it may mean that this is a relationship that cannot be ignored. There is soul work to be done.

Friendship

Today, it is possible to have many "friends" on Facebook. But what really constitutes friendship? Unlike *en*, friendship usually does not always involve some common project that brings two people together. Rather, friendship simply involves two people who care about each other and enjoy each other's company and look forward to that enjoyment. Friendship is often limited to a few individuals in a lifetime. In my life, friends have come from people I have worked with, but the importance of work in the relationship faded. Instead, I became interested in the other person's life.

Emerson ([1940] 1968) felt there were two elements to friendship. The first is truth. He wrote, "A friend is a person with whom I may be sincere. Before him I may think aloud" (228). There is no pretense; we feel relaxed and at home with a friend. The second element is tenderness. With our friends, we are kind; we practise *ahimsa* with a friend and make no effort to harm that person. Emerson writes, "The only way to have a friend is to be one" (234). At the end of his essay on friendship, he writes, "The essence of friendship is entireness, a total magnanimity and trust" (236).

French philosopher Michel de Montaigne also wrote about friendship. Friendship for Montaigne had its own inherent value unlike most other relationships, which are organized around some project or goal. Bloom (1993) writes that this view of friendship "is like happiness, which can never be supplemented because it contains all good things … In a sense, Montaigne argues that friendship is happiness, and is therefore desired for its own sake and with no need for anything beyond it" (421). Friendship is mutual and reciprocal. Montaigne's view of friendship is idealistic, and was based on his close friendship with Étienne de La Boetie.

We have seen through the work of Carroll (2014) that romantic relationships and marriage require work and effort to blossom into wholehearted relationships. Friendship may not require the same level of effort, but it does ask for the things that Emerson ([1940 1968] writes about – truth, tenderness, and trust.

In his book, *To Be a Friend: The Key to Friendship in Our Lives*, David Hunt (2010) describes various ways that we can enrich our friendships. The book presents a set of activities that form a workshop approach to being a friend. Hunt begins his book with the Golden Rule of Friendship: "Let me be a friend to others as I would have them be a friend to me" (21). He offers this definition but encourages readers "to make it their own." Each person needs to develop his or her language in working with the Golden Rule of Friendship. Hunt outlines five major principles in being a friend:

- Being a Friend Means to Be Friends with Yourself
- Being a Friend Means Accepting the Other Person
- Being a Friend Means Honouring Friendship Ties
- Being a Friend Means Welcoming the Spirit of Friendship
- Bring Out Your Meaning of Friendship: Your Meaning Map. (68–9)

I have already discussed the first principle in chapter 2 and cited some of Hunt's ideas there. Regarding the second principle, Hunt (2010) makes the distinction between acceptance and agreement. Hunt would like to offer friendship to people he may not agree with. To do this, he tries to set aside his own beliefs when listening to someone; then, he can accept someone without necessarily agreeing with them. Here Hunt focuses on the person's humanity so that there can be some feeling of connection. He makes it clear that this is not easy, and writes that in the "rare instances where I maintained the courage to do so, I have always been rewarded by learning more about them and more about myself" (72). He approaches each person without any expectation of personal gain, only the wish to be a friend, "that's all" (72). Critical to this process is giving full attention to the other person when they are talking. This almost always gives the person to whom you are listening "the feeling of being a worthy person" (72). This second principle includes making space for others. Hunt does this through letting go of his ego. Again, not an easy thing to do, but the effort is essential to begin a friendship.

The third principle is honouring friendship ties. As a friendship develops, so do the expectations. These may include how often you meet or communicate with the friend or something deeper, such as trust. However, over time people in friendships can change, and with that expectations may also change. So Hunt (2010) in his relationships makes the effort to change to keep the relationship strong. To do so, he will ask the question, "Will my actions help or hinder the relationship?" (76). For example, should one always be honest, particularly if honesty can be hurtful? Emerson ([1940] 1968) wrote about truth and tenderness in friendship, and often we must find the right balance between these two elements.

Hunt (2010) suggests that the fourth principle, being a friend means welcoming the spirit of friendship, is the most important. The spirit of friendship is the mystical element that underlies friendship. We cannot control the ebb and flow of a relationship, and we need to honour this aspect of friendship. For Hunt this means acting from his heart and trusting his underlying spirit, which "involves the warm and gentle flow of affection" (77).

The fifth principle is making your own meaning map. This involves how you perceive friendship through "its sound, sight, touch and other senses; how you feel when you experience friendship; how you express friendship through your actions; and how you express it in your thoughts through words" (Hunt 2010, 77).

Hunt (2010) then presents a variety of activities through which to explore each of these principles. These activities can be used with adults and adapted for working with adolescents and older children. Here is one exercise that explores the nature of friendship through the senses. It starts with sound:

> SOUND. What is the sound of friendship? Is there a tone of voice that reminds you of being a friend? Are there sounds in nature that you associate with friendship? What about sounds in your daily life; anything there that reminds you of being a friend? Is there a song or a musical piece that you associate with friendship? How about musical instruments? (174)

The exercise then focuses on sight, touch, smell, taste, feeling, body sensations, action, words, time, place, and people. With each of these we are asked to see what arises when connected to friendship. Hunt's book is both a practical and inspiring guide to friendship. He shares a lot of his personal experiences with being a friend.

Metta

Metta is the Pali word for lovingkindness. It can also be translated as friendliness. It is possible to live a life of metta where we extend friendliness to all beings. This will be discussed more fully in the next chapter, but in adopting metta, we approach each person we meet with a basic stance of openness and kindness. We are not afraid to smile at someone we do not know. Recently, I was on train and sitting directly across from a young man with a beard. We did not look each other when I first sat down. However, after about thirty minutes, we looked at each other and we both smiled. It was a wonderful moment. Just passing someone on the street and exchanging hellos can make your day. There are plenty of opportunities to practise metta during the day – with the checkout person at the grocery store, the bus driver, and colleagues at work.

The Greeks believed in extending friendliness to strangers. This was called *xenia* and was inspired by the Greek conception of the gods, whom they felt intervened in the lives of people. Thus a stranger coming to one's door could be a god in the guise of a person. There was also a practical reason for extending friendship and hospitality to strangers, as it created a tradition of reciprocity between the host and the stranger; thus when the host was travelling, he or she might expect the same generosity from others when away from home (Phillips 2007, 141).

Xenia is a central theme in Homer's *Odyssey*. Odysseus travelled for years and often depended on the kindness of strangers to survive during his long ordeal. When he returned home he did so as a stranger who was not recognized by his wife and her suitors. They believed that he had died. The suitors had transgressed against *xenia* as they were rude and continued to stay after they were asked to leave. In the end, Odysseus killed all the suitors and this, in part, was punishment for not fulfilling their responsibilities towards *xenia*.

Some Indigenous peoples such as the Sioux believe that there are really no strangers on the planet as all beings, including the animals, come from the womb of Mother Earth.

Today, *global education* attempts to see all human beings on the planet as connected to one another and not as strangers. Schools have programs where students write to pen pals in other countries or communicate with them over the Internet. It could be argued that the Internet is helping create McLuhan's global village, in which there are fewer strangers.

Embodiment

Whatever the form of personal love, the physical presence of the other is crucial. Sherry Turkle (2015), who has done research on empathy, has found that "without conversation, studies show that we are less empathic, less connected, less creative and fulfilled" (13). Turkle is not talking about conversations on the Internet but those that are face to face. Of course, Skyping can help us sustain communication, but if the discussion becomes difficult, it is too easy to sign off. When we are face to face, it is more difficult to walk away. The presence of the other person can help us work through difficulty. Turkle cites the research of Daniel Siegel who found that children need eye contact to develop the part of the brain that is involved in attachment. "Repeated tens of thousands of times in the child's life, these small moments of mutual rapport [serve to] transmit the best part of humanity – our capacity for love – from one generation to the next" (171). Eye contact is also part of what Turkle calls "whole person conversation" where we engage each other fully. Barbara Fredrickson (2014), whose research was described in the first chapter, writes, "Physical presence is key to love, to positivity resonance" (25). The importance of presence will be discussed more fully in chapter 8.

Educational Applications

The work of Linda Carroll (2014) and the stages of relationship could be examined and discussed by older adolescents as they start to engage in romantic relationships. Seeing the complexity of relationships could help young people navigate loving relationships. Reading about the soulful quality of relationships is also important as students can see how mystery is part of romantic involvement.

The work of David Hunt (2010) could provide the basis for discussing the nature of friendship. In the day of Facebook, students need to examine the nature of friendship. What is involved in being a good friend? There are important issues around being a friend that young people can discuss. Another issue to examine is the role of technology in making friends. The work of Sherry Turkle (2015) could also provide a framework for this discussion.

Finally, using metta as a way to approach meeting others could also be discussed. What does it mean to adopt such an approach in one's life? This discussion can even move beyond one's personal life to social issues such as immigration.

4

Impartial Love: Compassion and Lovingkindness

"If you practice true love, very soon that love will grow and include all of us."
– Thich Nhat Hanh

Ecology has shown us one of the fundamental realities of existence – interconnectedness. In nature everything is immersed in the web of life. Fritjof Capra (1996) argues that "deep ecological awareness is spiritual or religious awareness ... when the individual feels a sense of belonging, of connectedness, to the cosmos as a whole, it becomes clear that ecological awareness is spiritual in its deepest essence" (7). Einstein (cited in Wilber, 1984) spoke of a cosmic religion, which involves an awareness of the harmony of nature and our desire to be part of that harmony:

> The individual feels the sublimity and marvelous order which reveal themselves both in nature and in the world of thought. Individual existence impresses him as a sort of prison and he wants to experience the universe as a single significant whole. (102)

Interconnectedness and interdependence also lie at the heart of Buddhism. For example, Thich Nhat Hanh (1993) talks about *interbeing* which also refers to how deeply life is interconnected. When we see this interconnectedness, compassion for ourselves and others can arise. When the Dalai Lama looks out at an audience, he sees people who desire happiness and to be free from suffering. Happiness here is not just a temporary sense of well-being but includes a deep sense of connection.

Mahatma Gandhi (1980) believed that there is basic unity to life. He said,

> The forms are many, but the informing spirit is one. How can there be room for distinctions of high and low where there is this all-embracing fundamental unity underlying the outward diversity? For that is a fact meeting you at every step in daily life. The final goal of all religions is to realize this essential oneness. (63)

Gandhi's position, that this unity is evident in everyday life, reflects the notion that the interconnectedness of reality should not be relegated to remote forms of mysticism. Gandhi's commitment to nonviolent action arose from this understanding, which will be discussed more fully in chapter 7.

If we are truly interconnected, then we can naturally feel compassion for others. Compassion means that we truly feel the suffering of others and attempt to relieve that suffering where possible. Mathieu Ricard (2015) writes about this: "Altruism and compassion have the aim of spreading themselves as widely as possible. We must simply understand that our own wellbeing and the world's cannot rest on indifference to the happiness of the other or on a refusal to care about the sufferings around us" (24).

Ricard (2015) also makes the distinction between empathy, compassion, and lovingkindness. He defines empathy as "the ability to enter into affective resonance with the other's feelings and to become cognitively aware of his situation" (26). Empathy can alert the person to the sufferings of others and "catalyzes the transformation of altruistic love into compassion" (26). Compassion is concerned with ending suffering while lovingkindness focuses on sending thoughts of well-being to others. Impartiality is essential to lovingkindness and compassion. Ricard writes that it is similar to the physician who treats anyone who is ill that comes and does not discriminate or favour one person over another. The rays of the sun have been used as a metaphor here as they reach all beings equally.

Ricard (2015) does distinguish between *instinctive* altruism and compassion and *extended* compassion. The former arises naturally; for example, a mother's love for her child. Extended compassion, however, is impartial and needs to be cultivated. Here we see that others, who may come from different cultures, have the same needs as those close to us. Both instinctive and extended compassion require both an emotional and cognitive component. The cognitive element involves seeing the causes of suffering. Only by seeing deeply into the situation will one begin to recognize the conditions that give rise to suffering, and it is these conditions that must be addressed.

Ricard (2015) also makes the case that our happiness and the happiness of others are connected. When we are caring of others, it can engender a sense of well-being or "feeling of harmony with ourselves" (82). He cites Plato who said, "The happiest man is he who has no trace of malice in his soul" (82). Ricard goes on to argue that "love, affection, and concern for others are, in the long run, essential to our survival" (82).

We now turn to empathy, lovingkindness, and compassion and how they can be nurtured in educational settings.

Empathy

Empathy refers to our ability to put ourselves in another person's shoes. Like compassion, it has both affective and cognitive components. We can either feel what another person is experiencing or have some cognitive understanding of what is happening to another. C. Daniel Batson's (2009) research on empathy has identified eight different forms. The one that is relevant to this discussion is what he calls *empathic concern*, which involves becoming aware of another person's needs and wanting to help that person. This form of empathy is close to compassion and allows us to eventually become compassionate. Ricard (2015) writes about the connection between empathy and compassion:

> These three dimensions – love of the other, empathy (which is resonance with another's suffering), and compassion – are naturally linked. When altruistic love encounters suffering it manifests as compassion. This transformation is triggered by empathy, which alerts us to the fact that the other is suffering. One may say that when altruistic love passes through the prism of empathy, it becomes compassion. (58)

Roots of Empathy is a unique program developed by Mary Gordon (2005) for elementary school children. Gordon defines empathy as similar to Batson's empathic concern. She writes that "empathy is frequently defined as the ability to identify with the feelings and perspectives of others. I would add *and to respond appropriately* to the feelings and perspectives of others" (30, emphasis in original). Her program involves bringing a mother with her baby into a classroom over an entire school year. A Roots of Empathy instructor accompanies the child into the classroom as well. The students witness and identify with the growth of the baby during that period. The process of learning empathy comes in the following manner. First, students observe the baby's experiences and the emotions the baby inspires. Second, students learn to identify the emotions, and "anchor the emotions in themselves privately through discussion, reflection, art and journaling" (125). Finally, they can talk about their feelings with other students.

Gordon (2005) gives several examples of how this program has reached the most challenging students, such as this one:

> Darren was the oldest child I ever saw in a Roots of Empathy class. He was in grade 8 and had been held back twice. He was two years older than everyone else and already starting to grow a beard. I knew his story: his mother had been murdered in front of his eyes when he was four years old, and had lived in succession of foster homes ever since. Darren looked menacing because he wanted us to know he was tough: his head was shaved except for a ponytail at the top and he had a tattoo on the back of his head.
>
> The instructor of the Roots of Empathy program was explaining to the class about the differences in temperament that day. She invited the young mother who was visiting the class with Evan, her six-month-old baby, to share her thoughts about her baby's temperament. Joining in the discussion, the mother told the class how Evan liked to face outwards when he was in the Snugli and didn't want to cuddle into her, how she would have preferred to have a more cuddly baby. As the class ended, the mother asked if anyone wanted to try on the Snugli, which was green and trimmed with pink brocade. To everyone's surprise, Darren offered to try it, and as the other students scrambled to get ready for lunch, he strapped it on. Then he asked if he could put Evan in. The mother was a little apprehensive, but she handed him the baby, and he put Evan in, facing towards his chest. That wise little baby snuggled right in and Darren took him into a quiet corner and rocked back and forth with the baby in his arms for several minutes. Finally, he came back to where the mother and the Roots of Empathy instructor were waiting and he asked: If nobody has ever loved you, do you think you could still be a good father? (6)

Gordon (2005) goes on to comment that the openness and uncritical affection of a baby can lead to transformation in children. The parent–child relationship can be a model for loving relationships and children respond to what Gordon calls "the wisdom of the baby." The emotions of the baby are spontaneous and pure and have not been socialized into the masks that we tend to wear as adults. Gordon writes, "Children who have felt alienated or excluded are drawn into a circle of inclusion through the empathic contact made by the baby" (7).

Dr Kimberly Schonert-Reichl from the University of British Columbia has done research on the Roots of Empathy program and found that children who experienced the program were more advanced in their emotional and social understanding than students who had not experienced the program (Gordon 2005, 246).

Lovingkindness

Lovingkindness, or metta, was briefly discussed in the last chapter; it involves extending our wishes of well-being to ourselves and others. Sharon Salzberg (1995) is one of the most respected teachers of metta. She writes:

> Metta – the sense of love that is not bound to desire, that does not have to pretend that things are other than the way they are – overcomes the illusion of separateness, of not being part of a whole. Thereby metta overcomes all of the states that accompany this fundamental error of separateness – fear, alienation, loneliness, and despair – all of the feelings of fragmentation. In place of these, the genuine realization of connectedness brings unification, confidence, and safety. (21)

Metta can be seen in a steady attitude of friendliness: "The culmination of metta is to become a friend to oneself and all of life" (Salzberg 1995, 25). Metta, then, is ultimately a meditation on how we are connected to people, animals, life, and all creation.

Metta meditation can be done either as a meditation in itself or combined with other meditations. For example, it can be done at the beginning or end of a meditation period. It can also be done during the day while standing in line, riding the bus, or doing some other activity that does not demand total attention. The essence of this meditation is to centre on the heart area and to contact a basic warmth there. After connecting with the heart area, attempt to share this warmth and energy with others. There are various forms of lovingkindness and the one below was taught to me by a Burmese monk, U Silananda. I have made some minor changes in the wording.

> May I be well, happy, and peaceful.
> May my family be well, happy, and peaceful.
> May my friends be well, happy, and peaceful.

May my neighbours be well, happy, and peaceful.
May my colleagues be well, happy, and peaceful.
May all people that I meet be well, happy, and peaceful.
May all people that I am having difficulty or feel anger towards be well,
    happy, and peaceful.
May all beings on this planet be well, happy, and peaceful.
May all beings in this universe be well, happy, and peaceful.

This approach starts with those who are emotionally closest to us
and then moves out from there. Another approach is to move out
geographically.

May I be well, happy, and peaceful.
May all beings in this room be well, happy, and peaceful.
May all beings in this building be well, happy, and peaceful.
May all beings in this neighbourhood be well, happy, and peaceful.
May all beings in this town or city be well, happy, and peaceful.
May all beings in this region be well, happy, and peaceful.
May all beings in this hemisphere be well, happy, and peaceful.
May all beings in this planet be well, happy, and peaceful.
May all beings in this universe be well, happy, and peaceful.

When you are doing this lovingkindness meditation, it is also possible
to visualize the people that you are sending these thoughts to. I start my
classes with this exercise and I find that it adds immeasurably to the tone
and feel of the class. Many of my students have commented on it as well.

Another approach to lovingkindness practice is to focus first on a person that you feel close to. You imagine the person and then send thoughts
such as:

May you be free from suffering.
May you be healthy.
May you be free from danger.
May you dwell in wisdom.
May you dwell in compassion.
May you rejoice in the happiness of others.

You can choose any words that you feel are appropriate. After focusing on someone you feel close to, you can choose someone that is more

neutral in terms of your feelings. Again, imagine that person and send these thoughts of well-being to him or her. Finally, you can choose a person that you are having difficulty with or feel anger towards. This can be challenging and should not be undertaken if your negative emotions are still very strong.

Although this practice comes from the Buddhist tradition, I believe it is universal in nature. As I mentioned, I start my classes with a lovingkindness meditation. I have had students from all the major faiths in my classes and, in my twenty-four years of using it, no one has objected or felt that he or she could not participate.

In the Buddhist teachings, the outcomes of lovingkindness practice include:

1. You will sleep easily.
2. You will wake easily.
3. You will have pleasant dreams.
4. People will love you.
5. Devas [celestial beings] and animals will love you.
6. Devas will protect you.
7. External dangers [poisons, weapons, and fire] will not harm you.
8. Your face will be radiant.
9. Your mind will be serene.
10. You will die unconfused.
11. You will be reborn in happy realms. (Salzberg 1995, 41)

Many of my students have reported a "more serene mind" and "sleeping more easily" after doing this practice. Research is now beginning to focus on lovingkindness practice. One study found that kindness increased among those university students who were taught this practice compared to a control group in which the students' imaginings were neutral (Hutcherson, Seppala, and Gross 2008).

Qualitative Study on Teachers Who Did Lovingkindness Practice

Keith Brown (2017) has recently completed a master's thesis studying teachers' use of lovingkindness practice to send thoughts of well-being towards their students. Four teachers participated in the study: three from elementary schools and one who was teaching adult learners. Brown considers metta practice to be similar to prayer, and his study centred on the question of whether this practice actually could "create intersubjective connection with others." He was also interested in whether the practice encouraged the development of empathy.

> As I embarked on this study, I felt a need to understand how imagining others authentically relates to the ability to empathize with students in real time situations, as well as how effectively the practice can foster a curiosity toward learning the needs of others. I was particularly intrigued by the question of whether a solitary practice of recitation or meditation could foster the wish to understand others and put oneself in the place of students in a stressful classroom. (181)

Brown (2017) started with the lovingkindness phrases outlined above but changed the words slightly to "may my students be well, happy, and peaceful" and "may my classrooms be well, happy, and peaceful." The participants did the lovingkindness practice for three weeks and at the end wrote their reflections. Brown also interviewed the participants. The study had several interesting findings.

One was *embodied presence* in the classroom. One participant, David, noted that the practice made him calmer. David wrote this in his reflections:

> I noticed that there were many sessions (more during week 2 and 3) where I began to feel more calm and at peace during and immediately after the meditation. During the meditation, I remember feeling sensations in my feet and legs. The feeling was soothing and I also felt sensations in my chest and my face/mind felt very relaxed. I found it very beneficial to feel this way (of calmness) right before I had to teach my next class, which happened to be my most challenging one. And because of this feeling of calmness, I felt I was more patient, relaxed, and overall more effective with everyone I had to deal with at school. (Brown 2017, 182–3)

Brown points out that the practice let David be more fully present in the classroom and be more patient with his students. Another participant, Jill, found the practice helped her move away from perfectionism. She said that the practice helped her not to worry as much about her teaching and that she got "more peaceful and happy with everything" (183). Another participant, Karen, noted that through the practice "a caring identity" emerged (184). Brown speculates that because the practice allowed her to relax more, this caring was something that revealed itself rather than being built or created.

Another finding was that teachers moved away from seeing themselves as authorities in the classroom to seeing "their students as equally valid sources of learning and knowledge" (Brown 2017, 186). One participant, Nicole, began to see the relationships with students as more of a human relationship rather than a teacher–student relationship. Brown (2017) concludes:

> It seems that Loving Kindness Meditation creates a space for teachers to suspend their traditional caregiver and "teacher" role, as well as appreciate the students as human beings with their own unique interests and tendencies. For this reason, I feel that the emphasis of Loving Kindness Meditation is not on the wishing intention itself but on the perspectives of others, and giving a space for others to be authentically themselves. Interestingly, reciting loving-kindness also had the converse effect of allowing teachers' authentic selves to emerge, rather than being stifled by the role of teacher. (187)

Brown (2017) also found that doing lovingkindness practice created certain tensions. Sometimes the teacher could create an *ideal model* of what relationships should be in the classroom, which could not be met. Brown writes, "While teachers can wish their students wellness, that wishing doesn't necessarily translate to a smoothly running relationship with the student, let alone to students' reciprocating that well-wishing in turn" (187).

Brown (2017) goes on to theorize about the role of Eros in education. He writes:

> Loving Kindness Meditation did not limit Eros to a reciprocal experience with students but, instead, allowed teachers to find intrinsic values in developing compassion toward their students, including a greater appreciation of their students and ability to manage anxiety and anger. In this sense, the teachers were also no longer restricted to their physical position as teachers, but were, more so, able to reimagine themselves through the imaginative framings of Loving Kindness. (190)

Brown (2017) also found that a variety of emotions, including anxiety and fear, could arise during lovingkindness practice. Some of the teachers had difficult students, so that when they recited the lines of the practice, anger could arise. Over time the practice allowed the teachers to accept whatever they were feeling rather than trying to manipulate what they were experiencing.

But while many emotions arose as the teachers recited to their students, framing Loving Kindness Meditation as a spiritual practice itself paradoxically gave the teachers a contemplative space not to judge those emotions or react immediately to them. Over time, the teachers learned to refrain from suppressing difficult emotions toward their students, to the point where they no longer pushed themselves to fulfill a stereotypical loving or caring role. Consistently returning to a spiritual practice gave the teachers time to nurture and cultivate a loving disposition, rather than leaving it up to chance or the occasional reflection. (193)

Lovingkindness practice allowed a "gentle opening to the unknown." Brown (2017) cites the work of Fidyk (2009), who suggests the need to "bring eros and pedagogy into an appropriate, balanced relation without diminishing either" (62) and that lovingkindness practice can help in this process. At the end of his paper, Brown (2017) reflects on how meditation is not just "looking inward" but allows him "to see loving energy in all beings around me. This feeling is not a passionate, euphoric rapture for me, but more of a general sense that I don't need to retreat into my own solitary thoughts to find where I am" (197).

Although Brown's study was limited to four participants who did the practice for three weeks, it explores the many potential dimensions of lovingkindness practice in teaching. It is a very rich study that makes an important contribution to the role of love in teaching and learning.

Lovingkindness and Nonviolent Change

Aung San Suu Kyi, who has been the leader of the democratic reform movement in Burma for the past thirty years, believes that metta has been central to the change that has occurred there. Her political work is clearly in the tradition of Gandhian nonviolence. Peter Popham (2012) writes that for Suu Kyi "non-violence was a must" (116). He compares her to Gandhi in that she has the same quality of embodying the democratic hopes of her country as well as its "pride, its courage, its community – transcending sol-idarity, its will to shake off centuries of tyranny and reinvent itself" (371). Meditation has been central to her political work. Popham makes the point that her practice of metta, or lovingkindness meditation as taught by U Pandita, was crucial to her development as a leader. Before she started her practice, she was harshly critical of the head of the Burmese government, U Ne Win, and accused him of causing "the nation to suffer for 26 years" (296). Popham writes, "If she had listened to U Pandita before making that speech, those harsh words against the tyrant might have gone unsaid" (296). Popham speculates that she might have avoided arrest at that time with more compassionate words.

Suu Kyi (1997) talks about the importance of compassion in her work:

> We put a great emphasis on *metta*. It is the same idea as in the biblical quotation: "Perfect love casts out fear." While I cannot claim to have discovered "perfect love," I think it's a fact that you are not frightened of people whom you do not hate. Of course, I did get angry occasionally with some of the things they did, but anger as a passing emotion is quite different from the feeling of sustained hatred or hostility. (163)

Metta is also the founding principle of her party, the National League for Democracy (NLD). When asked about the founding principle, she said:

> It is metta. Rest assured that if we should lose this metta, the whole democratic party would disintegrate. Metta is not only to be applied to those that connected with you. It should be applied to those who are against you. Metta means sympathy for others. Not doing unto others what one does not want done to oneself ... So our league does not wish to harm anyone ... We are an organization that is free from grudge and puts metta to the fore. (Cited in Popham 2012, 312)

Suu Kyi has been criticized as "the perfect hostage" in that her stance of nonviolence seemed to be leading nowhere (Wintler, 2008). With the movement towards a democratic Burma, Popham (2012) argues that not only has her nonviolent stance changed Burma but it has also "changed the world" (388). Popham writes, "Suu changed Burma by throwing open the windows of her stale and stagnant homeland and letting the winds of the world blow in" (388). Suu Kyi sees what is happening in Burma as a model for other countries in Asia that are struggling for democracy. Her work has had an impact on Gene Sharp (2012), who has written an important book on nonviolence entitled *From Dictatorship to Democracy: A Conceptual Framework for Liberation*, originally published in 1993. This book has been translated into twenty-eight languages and describes nonviolent change that has occurred around the world. It has inspired nonviolent activists, including the Serbian activist group called Otpor (Resistance), whose nonviolent protests led to the downfall of Milošević in 2000. Sharp's book was first inspired by his visit to Burma and the impact of Suu Kyi's nonviolent stance. He met with many people there and, in Sharp's words, Suu Kyi's "heroism and inspiration" were fundamental to his book, which continues to inspire nonviolent movements around the world. This is the basis for Popham's (2012) claim that Aung San Suu Kyi has changed the world. It also shows the potential power of metta. Nonviolence as a form of love will be discussed more fully in chapter 7.

Compassion

It is almost impossible to speak about compassion today without mentioning Karen Armstrong (2010). She has devoted her life to working on compassion and started the Charter for Compassion, an umbrella group for people to engage in collaborative partnerships worldwide. Here is the text of the charter:

> The principle of compassion lies at the heart of all religious, ethical and spiritual traditions, calling us always to treat all others as we wish to be treated ourselves. Compassion impels us to work tirelessly to alleviate the suffering of our fellow creatures, to dethrone ourselves from the centre of our world and put another there, and to honour the inviolable sanctity of every single human being, treating everybody, without exception, with absolute justice, equity and respect.
>
> It is also necessary in both public and private life to refrain consistently and empathically from inflicting pain. To act or speak violently out of spite, chauvinism, or self-interest, to impoverish, exploit or deny basic rights to anybody, and to incite hatred by denigrating others – even our enemies – is a denial of our common humanity. We acknowledge that we have failed to live compassionately and that some have even increased the sum of human misery in the name of religion.
>
> We therefore call upon all men and women ~ to restore compassion to the centre of morality and religion ~ to return to the ancient principle that any interpretation of scripture that breeds violence, hatred or disdain is illegitimate ~ to ensure that youth are given accurate and respectful information about other traditions, religions and cultures ~ to encourage a positive appreciation of cultural and religious diversity ~ to cultivate an informed empathy with the suffering of all human beings – even those regarded as enemies.
>
> We urgently need to make compassion a clear, luminous and dynamic force in our polarized world. Rooted in a principled determination to transcend selfishness, compassion can break down political, dogmatic, ideological and religious boundaries. Born of our deep interdependence, compassion is

essential to human relationships and to a fulfilled humanity. It is the path to enlightenment, and indispensable to the creation of a just economy and a peaceful global community. (https://www.charterforcompassion.org/images/ menus/charter/pdfs/CharterFlyer10-30-2012_0.pdf)

The Charter has been translated into thirty languages and it is estimated that two million people have signed it. Armstrong's work has led to cities and schools declaring that they are committed to the principles of the Charter. In her book, *Twelve Steps to a Compassionate Life*, Armstrong (2011) writes that "compassion can be defined, therefore, as an attitude of principled, consistent altruism" (9). The Golden Rule is the guide for acting compassionately, as it "asks us to look into our own hearts, discover what gives us pain, and then refuse under any circumstance whatsoever to inflict that pain on anybody else" (9). Armstrong identifies Confucius as the first person to develop the Golden Rule. The Chinese term *shu* is part of his conception and means people should avoid privileging themselves and "relate their own experience to that of others 'all day and every day'" (9). The goal for Confucius was to become a *junzi*, "a mature human being." Compassion then is related to our humanity and what it means to be a human being.

Compassion is also one of the four immeasurables identified by the Buddha. The others are *metta* (lovingkindness), *mudita* (sympathetic joy), and *upeksha* (equanimity). Lovingkindness was discussed above. Sympathetic joy is enjoying the happiness of others while equanimity means a steadiness of mind. Armstrong (2010) argues that, like Confucius, the Buddha believed there is natural goodness in the human being and the four immeasurables are inherent in us and need to be awakened.

All the major religions have some form of the Golden Rule, and Armstrong (2010) believes that compassion is the connecting thread between the various religions. She also cites recent research on the brain that supports the argument that compassion is part of our nature. One example is the recent discovery of mirror neurons that respond empathically when we witness the behaviour of someone else. Some neuroscientists believe that these are related to our empathic capacities.

There is also the research regarding the left and right brain. In her book *My Stroke of Insight*, Jill Bolte Taylor (2009), a brain scientist, describes her stroke experience and how it made her aware of the importance of right-brain thinking. Her stroke affected her left brain, which is the seat of logical thought and language. She refers to the "brain chatter" or that "calculating intelligence that knows when you have to do your laundry"

(31). It is also the home of our "ego center." In contrast, the right hemisphere sees things in relationship and in the large context of the whole. Taylor (2009) writes:

> ... our right mind perceives each of us as equal members of the human family. It identifies our similarities and recognizes our relationship with this marvelous planet, which sustains our life. It perceives the big picture, how everything is related, and how we all join together to make up the whole. Our ability to be empathic, to walk in the shoes of another and feel their feelings is a product of our right frontal cortex. (30)

Taylor (2009) also suggests that it is the place where we experience inner peace. For a period, her life was dominated by the right brain and here she experienced moments of deep peace and feelings of being connected to the cosmos. Before the stroke, like most people living in the industrialized world, Taylor was caught up in "do-do-doing lots of stuff at a very fast pace" (70). This stressful existence also led to frustration and anger. Her stroke allowed her to experience a different world. She writes, "In absence of my left hemisphere's negative judgment, I perceived myself as perfect, whole, and beautiful just the way I was" (74).

Through rehabilitation therapy, Taylor (2009) has recovered the use of her left brain, but she has learned to use both sides of the brain to live more fully and realize a deeper happiness. Now, when she begins to feel stressed, she "shifts right" and thus slows down and now listens to her body and trusts her instincts. She breathes deeply and repeats to herself, *"In this moment I reclaim my JOY, or In this moment I am perfect, whole, and beautiful, or I am an innocent and peaceful child of the universe*, I shift back into the consciousness of right mind" (178, emphasis in the original).

In *Twelve Steps to a Compassionate Life*, Armstrong (2010) identifies different ways to start living more compassionately. Using the twelve-step method from Alcoholics Anonymous, she suggests ways that we can overcome our egotism, which is rampant in modern society. She recommends that each step be done fully before moving on to the next step.

The first step is *learning about compassion*. Armstrong (2010) suggests reading the great teachers from the Axial Age (700 to 300 BC), which included "the Buddha, Confucius, Laozi, Isaiah, Ezekiel, Ezra, Socrates and Aeschylus," as well as the writers of the Upanishads (31). Compassion was central to their teachings. She also refers to the later teachings of Jesus and Muhammed. The second step is to *look clearly at the world today*. This means examining the strengths and challenges of different aspects of life, including the family, the workplace, education, and the nation as a whole. Is the Golden Rule being applied in each of these settings? Where does oppression exist? Armstrong calls on schools to "develop a curriculum to educate children in the importance of empathy and respect" (73). The third step is developing *compassion for yourself*, which involves some of the ideas presented in the second chapter of this book. She cites Albert Friedlander who believed that "if you cannot love yourself, you cannot love other people either" (75). Like David Hunt, Armstrong asks us to look at the positive aspects of ourselves as well as at our faults, which can include "the shadow" within each of us. She also agrees that we need to have a sense of humour in looking at ourselves. Armstrong suggests that meditation can be helpful in learning to be compassionate with ourselves. As we sit and witness the arising and passing of thoughts and different emotional states, we can develop a deep compassion for ourselves and also for others whom we understand likewise experience this constant flow of thoughts and emotions. Armstrong cites other teachers that can help us in the quest for living more compassionately, including Saint Paul:

> Love is always patient and kind; it is never jealous; love is never boastful or conceited; it is never rude or selfish; it does not take offence, and it is not resentful. Love takes no pleasure in other people's wrong doing but delight in truth; it is always ready to excuse, to trust, to hope, and to endure whatever comes. (I Corinthians 13:4–7)

The fourth step is *empathy*, which was discussed earlier in this chapter. Armstrong (2010) also recommends the lovingkindness practice described above, in which we learn to send thoughts of well-being to three individuals, moving from someone we like, then to a more neutral person, and finally to a person we have difficulty with. Armstrong recommends doing this practice every day, which she suggests develops "a capacity for inwardness and the ability to think of others in the same way as you think of yourself" (104). *Mindfulness* is the fifth step, and it will be discussed more fully in chapter 8. Armstrong's view of mindfulness is witnessing our everyday behaviour through paying attention to the present moment. Through mindfulness, "we can learn to live more fully in the present. Instead of allowing a past memory to cloud our present mood, we can learn to savor simple pleasures – a sunset, an apple, or a joke" (109). The sixth step is *action* where we apply what we learn from being mindful. Thus we become more aware of not saying something hurtful to another. Action is where we try to bring both the positive and negative version of the Golden Rule into our lives. In the former, we do something to others we wish for ourselves, and in the latter, we do not do something to others we do not want done to ourselves. She also suggests using the mindfulness to notice thought patterns that cause us suffering and, through that awareness, to gradually move away from them.

How little we know is the seventh step and begins the last half of Armstrong's (2010) program for living more compassionately. She cites Socrates as a person who questioned everything so that he and those he engaged realized the limits of their knowledge. This practice can lead to paradoxical moments of uncertainty but also to a place where wisdom can arise. Plato, Socrates's disciple, said that after such moments "does truth flash upon the soul, like a flame kindled by a leaping spark, and once it is born there it nourished itself hereafter" (120). Most spiritual practices involve an "emptying" where the ego is suspended so there can be awakening. The specific practices Armstrong suggests here are to recall moments of *ekstasis*, such as listening to music, and to recognize how language can fail us in describing the experience. Next she suggests examining your beliefs. Pick one opinion you have and then list the reasons for that opinion and those against. Armstrong asks, "Did you learn anything from such an examination particularly the critique?" (129). The third and final step is to recognize the mystery within yourself and others. This is a very important step in teaching as we try to honour the mystery in each student, even those who challenge us the most. The mystery within students can bring surprise and wonder into the life of the classroom if we can make room for it.

How should we speak to one another is the eighth step. Here Armstrong (2010) refers to Confucius who learned from his conversations with others. He conducted these with a softness so positions in the dialogue did not harden. Today, exchanges on Twitter and political debate lack the equalities that Confucius employed. Most important is deep listening, where we hear the words of a person as well as the tone of the voice and the body language. Also, we need to speak with care: "Do you get carried away with your own cleverness and deliberately inflict pain on your opponent?" (141).

Concern for everybody is the ninth step. This involves including strangers and people we do not know in our effort to be compassionate. We are living in time when nativist and exclusionary beliefs are arising around the world. Our compassion is being tested daily. Armstrong (2010) asks us to look behind the news to "the ordinary people who are affected by a crisis. Remember that they did not choose to be born into that part of the world" (150). She also suggests using a Buddhist exercise, which helps us see how everything in our lives has involved so many others. Everything from the clothes we wear to the food we eat involves countless people, often from distant countries.

Acquiring knowledge is the tenth step. Armstrong (2010) suggests that we should start by learning more about the history of different cultures and religions. She uses the example of Christians that have been quick to criticize Islam for terrorism and violence while not remembering the history of intolerance and violence in their own religion. She recommends picking one country or one religion to study and then learning as much as one can about that country or religion. This can involve reading an article or watching a movie connected to this country or religion. All of this needs to be done with the "science of compassion" (160).

The eleventh step involves *recognition*. Here we recognize our own role in relieving the suffering of others. Armstrong (2010) suggests identifying an image of someone suffering that moves us and to work with that image. Send thoughts of lovingkindness to that person and look for ways that you might help that person. For example, if we are moved by someone being tortured, we can become involved in Amnesty International.

The last step is *loving your enemies*. Martin Luther King Jr. said, "Hatred paralyzes life; love releases it. Hatred confuses life; love harmonizes it. Hate darkens life; love illumines it" (cited in Armstrong 2010, 183). Gandhi and King hated oppressive systems, but not individuals. They did not allow the poison of hatred to infect them. This is one of the reasons we still look to their teachings for guidance today. Armstrong (2010) suggests identifying a person whose behaviour you find difficult to accept and sending them thoughts of well-being: "This is the supreme test of compassion" (185). To help in this process, try to realize that this person is also suffering. No one escapes suffering and recognizing this can remove a barrier to compassion. I asked my meditation teacher, Norman Feldman, about how I could move away from being angry at George Bush when he was president. Norman said, "Remember he is suffering too."

Armstrong's program is a challenging one. Working with another person or a group could help support the process. These steps could also be used with youth in upper elementary and secondary schools. I believe Armstrong's (2010) approach could replace programs in character education. She ends her book with these lines:

A truly compassionate person touches a chord in us that resonates with some of our deepest yearning. People flock to such individuals, because they seem to offer a haven of peace in a violent, angry world. This is the ideal to which we aspire and it is not beyond our capacity. But even if we achieve only a fraction of this enlightenment and leave the world marginally better because we have lived in it, our lives will have been worthwhile. There is no more to be said. We know what we have to do. This is the end of the book but our work is just beginning. (193)

Charters for Compassionate Schools and Children

Armstrong's work has led to the new charters being published. One of these is the Charter for Compassionate Schools:

We – the students, teachers, staff, and parents of (*named place of learning*) declare our shared commitment to the following principles, and pledge to hold ourselves and one another accountable to their realization.

We recognize that every person shares a common humanity capable both of happiness and suffering. We pledge in our words and actions to treat everyone in this school community as we would wish to be treated, to help those around us who are in need, and to make amends when we cause another pain.

We recognize that we are a school with different abilities, body sizes, races, religions, classes, gender identities and sexual orientations. We pledge to step into the shoes of others and see how things look from their point of view, especially when we disagree or find ourselves in conflict

We recognize that intolerance and hatred cause suffering and that that when we stand by doing nothing, or laugh or post comments online when others bully, we contribute to the problem. We pledge to stand up to bullying and make this a school where everyone belongs.

In signing, we commit to practice the values in this Charter within our school community; in our daily interactions, whether teacher-to-teacher, teacher-to-student, or student-to-student; and in the projects we undertake within our community and in the world. (https://www.charterforcompassion. org/index.php/charter-for-compassionate-schools)

By the fall of 2016, seventy-five schools from around the world had signed the charter. Schools in Australia, Botswana, Canada, Egypt, Greece, India, Mexico, New Zealand, Netherlands, Pakistan, Spain, Uganda, United Kingdom, and the United States are participating. There are also ninety-four colleges and universities that have signed the charter.

There is also a Children's Charter for Compassion, which can be found at http://www.childrenscharterforcompassion.com/.

5

Love of Learning and the Importance of Curiosity

"Explore, and explore. Be neither chided nor flattered out of your position of perpetual inquiry."

– Ralph Waldo Emerson

"I have no special talents. I am only passionately curious."

– Albert Einstein

It is a common human experience to want to know and learn. This is most evident in babies and toddlers. We have all witnessed young children exploring their surroundings and asking questions about what they encounter. This activity is often accompanied by expressions of joy and delight. Susan Engel (2015) writes in her book on curiosity, "During the first three years of life, the urge to find out defines us" (6). Engel, like many others, observes that this urge seems to diminish over time, particularly in school. In her research she found most classrooms do not invite curiosity or love of learning. This continues despite the "overwhelming empirical support for the idea that when people are curious about something they learn more and they learn better" (7).

This chapter will explore curiosity and how it can be nurtured. As Engel (2015) notes, our desire to learn ranges over so many different areas and is one of the things that defines us as human beings:

> We want to know what happened before we were on earth, how people we've never met are living their lives, how a given building or machine was put together, what caused a friend to behave the way she did, and why a certain novelist stopped writing. Our appetite for knowledge crosses all time zones, geographic regions, and zooms in and out from the grand to the minute. (9)

As adults we also experience being immersed in learning. I love reading biographies and getting to know more about another human being. In 1982 I read my first biography of Emerson, and since then I have read his essays several times and have read several other biographies. Gandhi is another person that I cannot learn enough about. Sometimes our immersion in what we are doing leads to what Mihaly Csikszentmihalyi (1997) calls the flow experience. He describes the experience: "Self-consciousness disappears, yet one feels stronger than usual. The sense of time is distorted: hours seem to pass by in minutes" (31). Csikszentmihalyi also writes that the state of flow is also optimal for learning. The state of awareness that arises in flow helps the individual in acquiring new perspectives and skills.

Sean Pidgeon (2013), an editor and writer, refers to the state where our interest and curiosity take over as "rapturous research." He writes that it is "a state of enthusiasm or exaltation arising from the exhaustive study of a topic or period of history, the delightful but dangerous condition of becoming repeatedly sidetracked in following intriguing threads of information, or constantly searching for one more elusive fact" (n.p.). In writing a novel, he researched the origins of the King Arthur stories. He writes, "My novel became not so much a fictional exercise as a process of discovery. Every new and abstruse piece of evidence that I unearthed caused me – along with my fictional protagonist, a British archaeologist – to keep digging" (n.p.). The danger that he referred to in the quote above is knowing when to stop so that you are not overwhelmed with information. Still *rapturous research* is a wonderful metaphor for the *love of learning*. Instilling this love should be the goal of all teaching.

Kang and associates (2009) have done research that supports the idea of rapturous discovery. They found that when individuals pursue a question and are able to find answers, the part of their brain that registers pleasure is activated. Research suggests that the pleasurable experience of children who pursue inquiry helps support further exploration. Engel (2015) summarizes this finding, "learning feels good when the material satisfies curiosity, and such learning tends to last" (178).

Curiosity is what motivates us to learn more. Engel (2015) suggests that curiosity is often triggered by surprise or the unexpected. She gives the example of Elias Canetti, the 1981 Nobel Laureate for Literature, and his shock around an incident that took place in Vienna where a group of men had been acquitted of murdering workers there. A crowd gathered to object to the verdict, which led to police killing ninety people to stop the violence. The shock of reading about this event led Canetti to engage in extensive research about the event.

Ian Leslie (2014) argues that curiosity also takes us out of ourselves. It "reminds us that we are part of a far greater project, one that has been underway for at least as long as human beings have been talking to each other" (20). Leslie also believes that curiosity is a "crucial condition of feeling fulfilled and alive" (21). He cites research by Robert Wilson who found that people who did lots of reading and writing throughout their lives significantly slowed their rate of mental decline as they aged.

Curiosity takes two basic forms. One is a directed search for information and the other is more exploratory. The former is "goal oriented, utilitarian," and Engel (2015) gives the example of a person acquiring information for a trip to France. Exploratory curiosity does not have a specific goal and an example is when we end up surfing the Web, going from one item to another as our curiosity takes us to different places. These two approaches are related to what psychologists have termed *specific* and *diversive* curiosity. Diversive curiosity moves more quickly from topic to topic. Specific curiosity usually involves a sustained in-depth study of one particular topic – "furniture-making, the galaxy, the Russian revolution, the physiology of running, or the origins of tea" (14). Leslie (2014) uses the term *epistemic* for this type of curiosity and writes that it can be a "font of satisfaction and delight that provides sustenance for the soul" (17). Leslie believes there is a third form of curiosity that he calls *empathic* curiosity, which is about "the thoughts and feelings of other people" (18).

As noted above, surprise often motivates curiosity and learning. Novelty can draw us to inquire but exploring the unknown can also create anxiety. Nathan Fox and associates (2008) have found that temperament has a long-term effect on curiosity. Children with equanimity are less inhibited in exploring their surroundings than those children who become anxious.

Another important element in a child's curiosity is his or her attachment to an adult. If babies are secure in their relationship to their mothers, then they tend to be less inhibited in exploring the world around them than those children who are not certain about "the bond they have with their mother[s]" (Engel 2015, 32).

Free play and solitude also support curiosity. Both require time. Children's explorations are richer when they are not pressured by time (Fulton 2009). With time, children can develop a sense of autonomy. The Montessori classroom is designed to support this sort of autonomy (Lillard 2008). Play and solitude can eventually lead to a sense of agency in the child who can ask questions and then pursue ways to find answers. Gray (2013) has identified the main characteristics of play:

> (1) Play is self-chosen and self-directed; (2) play is activity in which means are more valued than ends; (3) play has structure or rules that are not dictated by physical necessity but emanate from the minds of the players; (4) play is imaginative, nonliteral, mentally removed in some way from "real" or "serious" life; and (5) play involves an active, alert, but non-stressed frame of mind. (140)

Unfortunately, the play that occurs in schools is often "supervised play" that has some sort of agenda.

Curiosity and Schools

Einstein wrote, "It is in fact nothing short of a miracle that the modern methods of instruction have not yet entirely strangled the holy curious of inquiry" (cited in Howe 2003, 134). Einstein's claim is supported by research. Tizard and Hughes (1984) studied the number of questions young children asked at home and at school. They found that at home they asked on average twenty-six questions per hour while at school the number dropped to two per hour. Engel (2015) studied the questions that children asked in a fifth grade classroom and found that teachers either ignored the children's questions or they were seen as off topic (91). She writes, "Mastery rather than inquiry seemed to be the dominant goal for almost all the classrooms in which we observed. Often it seemed that finishing specific assignments (worksheets, writing assignments) was an even more salient goal than actually learning the material" (95). Engel gives another example of a sophomore social studies class where a student asked a question about the American Revolution and the teacher answered, "I can't answer questions right now. Now it's time for learning" (100). Learning is seen by many teachers as following the textbook or the lecture.

Engel (2015) notes that curiosity requires ambiguity which teachers often avoid. There is evidence that curiosity supports learning and development so the teacher's efforts to cover the curriculum are barriers both to curiosity and learning (175). Children's development also influences their curiosity. In general, as children grow it becomes more focused and nuanced. Engel (2015) suggests that "curiosity becomes a narrower but perhaps brighter light, aimed with more intention" (104).

Frank Barron and David Harrington (1981) conducted a study of people who were creative and found that the only consistent variable was that they spent a lot of time out of school where they could pursue their own interests. Erik Erikson (1993) wrote about the importance of a "moratorium" during adolescence where youth have time to explore so that they could find their identity.

Progressive and child-centred educators such as John Dewey have argued that learning needs to be connected to the interests of the child. Material that is interesting to children catches their attention, which is also important to the learning process. Several studies have been done on reading and have found that the more interesting the text, the more the student understands and often reads the interesting material more quickly (Silvia, 2006; Knobloch et al. 2004). Of course, each child's interests vary. Judy DeLoache, Gabrielle Simcock, and Suzanne Macari (2007) studied young children and found that some children had "extremely intense interests" that last for long periods and are "self-perpetuating" (Engel, 111). Engel (2015) comments, "The more one knows about an interesting topic, the more one wants to know" (112). This leads to the *love of learning*. Engel goes on to assert that the connection between curiosity and knowledge is what leads to expertise. This absorption in a topic can also lead to cognitive advances in the child (112).

Engel (2015) asserts that "intellectual exotica" often interest children and can be used to stimulate learning in the classroom. She gives examples of teachers who use different ways of engaging children's interests. One example (Stigler and Stevenson, 1991) is where a teacher came into the classroom with a large paper bag and put it on her desk. Immediately the children were interested. The teacher then pulled out various containers, including a pitcher, a vase, and a beer bottle. This was an introduction to a lesson on measuring the volume of different containers. This is an example from Japanese classrooms where Stigler and Stevenson (1991) found that teachers used "mystery and uncertainty to organize their lessons" (120).

One method that almost always interests children is the use of stories. The sequence of the story and the plot carry the interest forward. The uncertainty of how a problem in the story will be resolved is usually the key to holding the students' interest. Growing up in the early days of television, there were many serials (e.g., *Don Winslow of the Navy*) that ran and each episode would conclude with some cliffhanger event that made me want to watch the next episode.

In school, Engel (2015) notes, storytime is the one time students are completely attentive to what the teacher is saying. In Waldorf education, stories are central to much of the learning that happens there. Teachers learn the art of storytelling in their teacher education. Warren Cohen and Brian Bresnihan (2017) write about how stories are used in the Waldorf curriculum:

> Listening to stories stills children outwardly while causing them to be quite active inwardly, creating images of unfolding events, feeling with the various characters, and anticipating what may come next. The art of storytelling is one of the important elements that brings the Waldorf curriculum to life. Not only do stories model organization of thought, sequencing of events, and the many varieties of personal relationships, they offer teachers an effective means for touching and teaching their students on the most profound levels. They go right to the heart.
>
> Stories foster a vibrant imagination that is important not only for developing creative expression, interpersonal skills, mental flexibility, and understanding others but equally for comprehending scientific concepts. Indeed, imagination is vital in every aspect of life. As children hear a story, they form pictures in their minds to go along with the words, yet each one sees something different. Shared stories are literally created anew within the imagination of each listener. As imaginations are stimulated, minds develop and become both more creative and more flexible.
>
> Whether a lesson is focused on language arts, history, geography, science, or mathematics, the starting point is most often "a story," fiction or nonfiction, biographical or historical, verse, poem, or song. The rest of the Waldorf curriculum rhythmically supports the story's content through interrelated lessons, reading, figuring, movement, artistic activities, direct experiences, and reflection on all the aforementioned. In this way, "the lesson," the content, is made whole and fully assimilated by each student in a rich, diverse, and integrated body of knowledge and experiences. (78)

Engel (2015) suggests that science has the element of wanting to find out what happens next when an experiment is conducted. She gives the example of a four-year-old on a walk with his grandmother who finds a bug on a leaf and wonders if the bug will eat the leaf. The grandmother simply replies, "Let's find out." Rather than giving an answer, the adult can say, "Let's wait and see what happens" (124).

At the end of her wonderful book on curiosity, Engel (2015) gives four recommendations for creating a curious classroom. The first is access to "books with good language and complex characters, fish tanks, terrariums, complex machines and gadgets and conversations about the unseen and unseeable" (190). An example of this comes from the Equinox Holistic Alternative School in Toronto. In one junior-level classroom, the year started with the installation of a salmon hatchery. The growth of the salmon during the year provided the basis for a number of activities in several different subjects. Math and science inquiry activities were developed around the salmon. One parent commented that this project brought all the subjects together. She said, "They were learning different subjects without realizing that they were learning. It was magical. I have seen the development of critical thinking, inquiry and love of learning" (Miller 2016, 294). The students also created a large mural around the salmon. Another parent commented, "They did art around salmon and they learned so much about salmon. It was so integrated – they wrote, they thought, they measured. What a beautiful, holistic thing. This was an incredible year and the kids did the salmon dance at the end of the year" (294). In the spring, the salmon were released into a nearby river. A documentary film was made of this project (for a discussion of the film, see Miller 2016).

The second recommendation is to develop the goal of question-asking so students learn to identify questions and then pursue them. Engel (2015) writes, "Teachers can develop activities that invite or require students to figure out what they want to know and then seek answers" (190). Students' questions are not dismissed but seen as opportunities for learning. A third recommendation is to give the students time to engage with their questions and provide resources when it seems appropriate. Engel acknowledges that assessing curiosity is a major challenge. One suggestion is to record the number of questions asked and how they are engaged. Audio and video recording can help in this process. This leads to the fourth recommendation, which is to analyse the questions that students raise so the "teachers can get ideas about how to help their students develop better questions" (192). These ideas can lead to new activities in the classroom.

The question remains, however, whether the current climate in education supports Engel's recommendations. With the lack of resources in many schools and accountability pressures, creating conditions for cultivating curiosity are difficult. Gray (2013), in his book on play, gives the example of the Sudbury Valley School in Massachusetts where the environment does support curiosity. Similar to A.S. Neill's (1997) Summerhill, the Sudbury Valley School allows children to follow their interests. Gray surveyed several graduates of the school and found that they were allowed to be responsible and self-directed in their studies. It is also a setting that fosters high motivation. Gray writes, "Their experience in a setting where learning had always been fun led them to want to continue learning. Moreover, most of the graduates reported that they had gone on to endeavors that they enjoyed and had chosen, and as a result their motivation was high" (95).

Gray (2013) describes some of the key elements of the Sudbury Valley School. The first one is time and space to play and explore; there is a lot of unscheduled time at the school. Engel (2015) has identified this as central to the development of curiosity. Another element at the school is access to knowledgeable and caring adults. The teachers do not act as remote authority figures and so students feel comfortable approaching them and asking them questions. Students also have access to "a wide range of the equipment that is of most use to people in our culture, including computers, cooking equipment, woodworking equipment, art materials, musical instruments, sports equipment of various types, and walls filled with books" (Gray 2013, 102).

Gray (2013) gives examples of several of the students who graduated from the Sudbury Valley School. Here is one:

> Carol, who went on to become a captain of a cruise ship, developed a love of boats during her time at Sudbury Valley. She played with small boats on the millpond located on the school's campus. As a teenager, she took advantage of the school's open campus policy to spend as much time as possible at a nearby seacoast area, where she studied navigation and sailing. (105)

Although Sudbury Valley is too unstructured for many parents, there is a need to explore how curiosity can be cultivated in a variety of educational settings. Leslie (2014) argues that curiosity also requires a large knowledge base, and he critiques programs like Sudbury Valley. My own position is that unless this knowledge base is presented in a way that engages students, there will be a lot of wasted energy on the part of teachers. Chapter 10 of this book describes the Equinox Holistic Alternative School in more detail and how it nurtures curiosity and the love of learning.

6
Love of Beauty

"Eros constantly kindles in us the flame of beauty and the desire for the Beautiful as a path towards growth and transformation."

– John O'Donohue

Beauty is rarely mentioned in education today. There is no place for the beautiful in the world of accountability and standardized testing. The one exception is Waldorf education, which will be discussed in the last part of this chapter. John O'Donohue (2004) argues, "The time is now ripe for beauty to surprise and liberate us. Beauty is a free spirit and will not be trapped within the grid of intentionality. In the light of beauty the strategies of the ego melt like a web against a candle" (7). Paradoxically, each person's expression of beauty is "individual and original … [Beauty] responds to the cry of the original voice" (81). When we hear someone speak with their original voice, inevitably we are moved. This voice can express itself in song, poetry, a few deeply felt words, or, again paradoxically, in silent presence. In his book *The Invisible Embrace: Beauty*, O'Donohue explores all dimensions of beauty and states that we seek it everywhere – "landscape, music, art, clothes, furniture, gardening, companionship, love, religion and in ourselves" (2). The experience of the beautiful can be like a homecoming. Music is one example of this homecoming. My grandmother introduced me to the music of Beethoven when I was a young boy and throughout my life his music, along with that of Mozart, Haydn, and Schubert, has been a beautiful home. I have had several experiences of hearing one of their pieces which I may not have not heard for long time and had a feeling of coming home.

We associate beauty with the arts but it has a place in science. Einstein believed there was sublime order to the universe. Walter Isaacson (2007), in his biography of Einstein, writes that music was a powerful influence on Einstein and was a "connection to the harmony underlying the universe. He was awed, both in music and physics, by the beauty of harmonies" (37). Einstein wrote that Mozart's music "is so pure and beautiful that I see it as a reflection of the inner beauty of the universe itself" (14). He also said that Mozart's music "is so pure it seems to have been ever present in the universe … Like all great beauty, his music was pure simplicity" (14).

From the ancient world, Plato (2006) wrote about love in several of his dialogues. Probably the most famous is the *Symposium* where Socrates converses with his colleagues about love. In this dialogue there is the rare appearance of a woman, Diotima. She presents the idea of a ladder of love proceeding from physical attraction to study the beauty of life and laws and the beauty of science. In the end the lover "comes to know just what it is to be beautiful" (211c). Socrates says that Diotima told him:

> The result is that he will see the beauty of knowledge and be looking mainly not at beauty in a simple example … but the lover is turned to the great sea of beauty, and, gazing upon this, he gives birth to many gloriously beautiful speeches, in unstinting love of wisdom, until having grown and been strengthened there, he catches sight of such knowledge, and it is the knowledge of such beauty. (210d)

In *Phaedrus*, Plato (2006) presents the image of how beauty awakens the soul. Here, Socrates refers to "the madness of a man, who on seeing beauty here on earth and being reminded of true beauty, becomes winged, and fluttering with eagerness to fly upward, but unable to leave the ground looks upwards like a bird, and takes no heed of things below – and that is what causes him to be regarded as mad" (249d5-e1). The "reminding" here is from the invisible world of the spirit that Plato believes we inhabit before birth. Here is Socrates's description of that world:

> But beauty was radiant to see at that time when the souls, along with the glorious chorus (we were with Zeus while others followed other gods), saw that blessed and spectacular vision and were ushered into the mystery that we may rightly call the most blessed of all. And we who celebrated it were wholly perfect and free of all the troubles that awaited us in time to come, and we gazed with rapture at sacred revealed objects that were perfect, and simple, and unshakeable and blissful. That was the ultimate vision, and we

saw it in pure light because we were pure ourselves, not buried in this thing we are carrying around now, which we call a body, locked in it like an oyster in its shell. (250b-c)

The remembering of this vision, then, can inspire the pursuit of beauty in this world. Emerson (2003) wrote, "The world exists to the soul to satisfy the desire of beauty ... Beauty, in its largest and profoundest sense, is one expression for the universe" (193). But Emerson goes on to write that this external beauty is "not ultimate. It is the herald of inward and eternal beauty, and is not along a solid and satisfactory good" (193). Like O'Donohue (2004), Emerson saw beauty as an autonomous force and writes that "beauty is the creator of the universe" (328). The poet represents beauty. Emerson (2003), in language reminiscent of Plato, writes:

So when the soul of the poet has come to ripeness of thought, she detaches and sends away from it its poems or songs – a fearless, sleepless, deathless progeny, which is not exposed to the accidents of the weary kingdom of time; a fearless, vivacious offspring, clad in wings (such was the virtue of the soul out of which they came) which carry them fast and far, and infix them irrecoverably into the hearts of men. These wings are the beauty of the poet's soul. (337)

The Earth's Beauty

While beauty is perceived through cultural and individual lenses, nature usually stands as something universally recognized as beautiful. Seeing the earth from space moved the astronauts and cosmonauts to describe the beauty they saw. Below are quotations from the book *Home Planet* (Kelley, 1988). The first is by Vladimir Lyakhov, and the second is by Charles Walker:

Although the ocean's surface seems at first to be completely homogeneous, after half a month we began to differentiate various seas and even different parts of oceans by their characteristic shades. We were astonished to discover that, during a flight, you have to learn anew not only to look, but also to see. At first the finest nuances of color elude you, but gradually your vision sharpens and your color perception becomes richer and the planet spreads itself before you with all its indescribable beauty. (65)

My first view – a panorama of brilliant deep blue ocean, shot with shades of green and gray and white – was of atolls and clouds. Close to the window I could see this Pacific scene in motion was rimmed by the great curved limb of the Earth. I had a thin halo of blue held close, and beyond, black space. I held my breath, but something was missing – I felt strangely unfulfilled. Here was a tremendous visual spectacle, but viewed in silence. There was no grand musical accompaniment, no triumphant inspired sonata or symphony. Each one of us must write the music of this sphere for ourselves. (18)

Native Americans, of course, have always been able to write this music. Ohiyesa, the Santee Dakota physician and author, wrote this:

Whenever, in the course of the daily hunt the red hunter comes upon a scene that is strikingly beautiful or sublime – a black thundercloud with the rainbow glowing arch above the mountain, a white waterfall in the heart of a green gorge; a vast prairie tinged with the blood-red sunset – he pauses for an instant in the attitude of worship. He sees no need for setting apart one day in seven as a holy day, since to him all days are God's. (Cited in McLuhan 1972, 36)

Beauty can evoke reverence and a sense of the sacred so missing today in modern society. As Vladimir Lyakhov stated, "We need not only to look but to see" (cited in Kelley 1988, 65). Thoreau (1961) also wrote about seeing: "I must walk more with free senses. It is as bad to *study* stars and clouds as flowers and stones … Be not preoccupied with looking. Go not to the object; let it come to you" (99). Through seeing, Thoreau was able to develop what he called "Beautiful Knowledge." He saw the relationships and connections in nature. Thoreau (2002) wrote: "The highest that we can attain to is not Knowledge, but Sympathy with Intelligence" (172). Beautiful Knowledge then includes empathy. His metaphor is the "lighting up of the mist by the sun." Thoreau used the sun as an image of that intelligence which is the source of "Beautiful Knowledge." At the end of the essay, "Walking," he writes:

So we saunter toward the Holy Land, till one day the sun shall shine more brightly than ever he has done, shall perchance shine into our minds and ears, and light up our whole lives with a great awakening light, as warm and serene and golden as on a bankside in autumn. (177)

This is a wonderful term, "Beautiful Knowledge," which can flower in educational environments where there is love.

Thomas Berry (1988) was a person who created such knowledge. His book *The Dream of the Earth* is an example of Beautiful Knowledge. For Berry, the ultimate reference point is the universe where interrelatedness is a central dimension. In this relatedness there is "mutual presence" of one element to another. The gravitational attraction that maintains this presence "finds its fulfillment in the meeting of individuals in the world of the living and in the full expression of affection at the level of human consciousness" (121). This affection, or love, leads to a *communion of subjects* rather than a collection of objects. Like Einstein, Berry sees an underlying unity in the universe. He refers to the curvature of the universe which is "closed to hold all things within an ordered pattern, while it is sufficiently open to enable the creative process itself to continue" (213).

The dream of the earth is the imagination that is in tune with this unfolding of the cosmos. The dream includes the magnificence of nature – "the shape of the orchid, the coloring of the fish in the sea ... the resonant croaking of the bullfrogs, the songs of the crickets, the pure joy of the predawn singing of the mockingbird" (Berry 1988, 197). Berry (1988) writes that this beauty inspired the creative imagination in Mozart's music, Dante's *The Divine Comedy*, and Shakespeare's plays and sonnets. These creations, along with so many others, come from the depth of our souls and from "the cosmic order itself" (197). How the merging of our psyches and the universe come together to create such wonders is a mystery. Emerson (2003) wrote that nature hates calculation and loves spontaneity. Berry (1988) refers to the *Tao Te Ching* in a similar manner. This is in accord with "Lao Tzu, the Chinese sage, who tells us that the human models itself on the earth, earth models itself on heaven, heaven models itself on tao, tao models itself on its own spontaneity" (196).

O'Donohue (2004) cites a quote from Keats that is relevant here: "I am certain of nothing but the holiness of the Heart's affection and the truth of Imagination ... whether it existed before or not – for I have the same Idea of all our Passions or Love they are all in their sublime, creative of essential Beauty" (148). After citing Keats, O'Donohue writes, "The passion of imagination is nourished from a deeper source, namely Eros" (149).

Waldorf Education

Beauty is central to Waldorf education. Waldorf educator Torin M. Finser (1994) had this Navajo poem recited in his third-grade class:

Beauty goes before me,
Beauty goes beside me,
Beauty follows me,
Mountains sing with me,
Bluebirds sing with me,
Tall pines talk with me,
I see the smoke coming from my Hogan,
My heart is good,
My spirit is good,
All is beauty. (59)

For the Waldorf teacher, art is not just a subject but is integral to almost everything in the curriculum. For Rudolf Steiner, the founder of Waldorf education, art was essential to the unfolding of the inner person. Mary Caroline Richards (1980) states that art involves "a certain way of seeing the child, a feeling for life, an intuition of the connections between the inner processes of forming and their outer expression ... A sense of awe rises in the presence of the child, as in the presence of a poem one hears forming in one's inner ear" (69). For Steiner, creative expression was linked with the cosmos itself. In his autobiography, he quoted a friend as saying: "People do not have as much as an inkling of the real significance of the creative power within the human soul. They do not realize that the creativeness of man is an expression of the same cosmic power that creates in nature" (cited in Wilson 1985, 72).

In discussing Waldorf education, it is important to be aware of the stages of human development that Steiner defined as the stages that form the basis for the curriculum. Each stage involves an awakening. The first stage (ages 0 to 7) is the awakening and development of the physical aspect of the person. The child begins to move his or her limbs, and so Waldorf education encourages children of this age group to move and clap their hands when learning to count. When learning to draw, the child uses large block crayons so that the colour can almost be felt as the child draws. In learning to draw forms and lines, the child's movement is also emphasized. Steiner believed that there were three main aspects of human existence: willing, feeling, and thinking. In getting the limbs to move, the will is exercised.

The next stage (ages 7 to 14) begins when the child's baby teeth give way to the adult teeth. In this stage, the focus of development is on feeling and imagination as development is centred in the heart and trunk area. It is important for the child to hear stories, fables, and legends that contain rich and meaningful images which nurture the child's inner imaginative life. The teacher is also important to this development, as Steiner felt that the student should have the same teacher through this period so a deep sense of trust can develop between teacher and child.

In the third stage (ages 14 to 21), the focus shifts to thinking, as the adolescent explores questions of meaning and is often attracted by ideas that can engage his or her passion. Artistic activity at this stage is integrated around the increasing intellectual concerns of the person.

The colour of the classrooms in a Waldorf school is aligned with the stage of development. In kindergarten and the primary years, the walls are painted in warm, nourishing colours such as pink, yellow, and red. By adolescence, when the energy of puberty arises, colours such as green and blue are used as a calming influence. There is great care given to what art is put on the wall. In the early years, there may be a picture of the Madonna and Child as it can have a warm, healing effect on the child.

Stephen Sagarin (1992) taught art at a Waldorf school and describes in detail how he approached the art class in grades 6 to 12. He states that art is not used to express "pent up" feelings but is seen as relating to "the development of children's capacity to observe and distinguish vital forces in nature and in themselves. The active experience of a creative idea is more essential than the art 'product' itself. The development of the student herself is key" (19).

In grade 6, Sagarin has students work with watercolours on paper that has been soaked in water for a few minutes and sponged dry. He asks the students to follow what he is painting but he does not tell them what the subject is. Eventually, the students discover the subject; however, by keeping the subject secret, the students begin to "see" the art in a different way. Sagarin (1992) states: "Rather than seeing in the conventional, undeveloped sense of what they think they see, they learn to see things as they are. All of what was merely a long, thin triangle may become a river" (20). Even though the students follow the teacher's lead, each picture comes out differently. The students use different brushes and different amounts of water in the colours. All this combines to give a unique effect.

Sagarin also has the students combine colours to form new colours. For example, blue and yellow are combined to make green. After mixing the colours, Sagarin asks the students if they think the colours are now balanced. If they feel the colour is too weak, they will add more blue to make the green stronger. Sagarin (1992) states: "By talking about the painting in terms of balance, the balance of light and dark, warm and cool, we approach a sense for colour harmony and discord" (20). According to Sagarin, some students prefer discordant paintings while others prefer more balance and harmony in the paintings. He begins the course with two colours but gradually adds others until there are six colours (three primary and three secondary). The rest of the colours the students must mix themselves.

The overall approach is based on the work of Johann von Goethe ([1810] 1970), who argues that colour arises from the interaction of light and dark. Goethe believes that the warm colours – red, orange, and yellow – arise when light passes through a darkening medium. The cool colours – blue and purple – arise when darkness is seen through a light-filled medium. Green appears when the two types of colour overlap. When the colours mentioned are painted around a circle, they form a colour wheel. Sagarin (1992) then describes how the colour wheel is used in the classroom:

> As the course progresses we often "step out" of the color wheel for a day or two to include black (a volcano erupting at night) or brown (an aqueduct over a sluggish, muddy river in the heat of a Roman summer). As much as possible, we paint scenes that arise from the student's main lesson study at the time of the course … Often this is the study of ancient Rome, although it can be the geography of the north (Tundra, fir trees, icy mountains, ice floes) or other subject. The point of the course is to deepen the children's capacity to see the world as a formation or product of color. (20–1)

The main lesson that Sagarin refers to is taught every morning for about two hours and usually focuses on a period of history or some story, legend, or myth. Students keep a book in which they draw or write. I have visited many Waldorf classrooms and the art that the students create in these books is always rich in colour.

In grade 7, the students study the Renaissance. According to Sagarin (1992), students at this age have a fascination with this period of history as they are intrigued by the possibilities of exploring and mastering many areas of endeavour simultaneously (e.g., music, sports, art, academics, drama). Linear perspective is taught within this context. Sagarin comments: "The world is open to them the way it was to the thinkers and explorers of the Renaissance. The discoveries of linear perspective challenge seventh graders, but they persevere readily. It's so 'cool' to able to draw buildings and roads that look 'real'" (21).

The class begins with focusing on how the "vanishing point" in a picture appears to move with the observer. Sagarin (1992) draws a road vanishing into the distance and the students follow the teacher's lead. Again, pictures differ as "some draw a dirt road with car tracks in it, while others draw a black asphalt strip with a double yellow line down the middle"

(21). Students also use light differently with some drawing the picture at midday while others focus on nighttime. Here, the students use coloured pencils for the work instead of watercolours.

In the next year, grade 8, one art project involves having the students make a model or caricature of the human face with clay or papier-mâché. Sagarin (1992) believes this process is helpful, as students in these grades are in the process of going through adolescence and are just finding out who they are. Sagarin comments: "By imaginatively creating, or re-creating the character of others, students begin the process of sorting out their own personalities" (21). In other subjects, students are studying the biographies of men and women in history and science, a process that allows them to reflect on the ways in which lives unfold. In preparing the model, the students first study the human face and its proportions. This process can lead to some insight on the subjectivity of our perceptions as students discover, for example, that the eyes are central in the head and not near the top as is the usual perception. The face is drawn from both the front and side. Various face forms are examined, including the masculine and feminine face, as well as stereotypes such as the intellectual or "egghead" or the sensitive "artiste."

After these explorations, the students start working with the clay to form a face. Three to five pounds are used, a mass ample enough to allow the students to shape the face with his or her hands, which renders the experience to be more direct and immediate. They start by forming a sphere and then gradually work on the features. Sagarin (1992) finds that a student's first efforts often reveal a face that is in many ways a self-portrait. For example, a student who sees herself as an intellectual will often make a high forehead while a student with low self-esteem will sculpt a face with an exaggerated, slack jaw.

Finally, Sagarin (1992) asks the students to express some emotion in the face such as "pain, sorrow, joy, boredom, curiosity" (22). After the students have expressed one emotion, Sagarin then asks them to do the opposite emotion. He says: "It is certainly good for someone who is melancholic to immerse himself in modelling some melancholic expression (which he will usually choose to) and then to have to model the opposite – either great joy or fiery intensity" (22).

By grade 9, students tend to see things in terms of black and white, just as they tend to the extremes of either love or hate. The Waldorf school allows the students to explore this tendency in art through black and white. Sagarin (1992) has them make block prints, which are black and white, but also allows the opportunity to reconcile the polarities. Sagarin also encourages the students to select something from the natural world to work with, such as a human or an animal. These objects are also drawn in their natural surroundings.

Sagarin's students start with line drawings before doing the block prints. This way, they can explore more freely the relationship between black and white and light and dark. He also encourages them to look at the work of other artists, such as Dürer and Picasso. Both artists worked at times in wood block prints but produced very different works. Picasso chose to distort the natural through his particular artistic vision while Dürer managed to produce almost photographic results, such as his famous woodcut of a hare in which it is said that "you can see every hair." In working with the wood, the students cannot erase lines, so they must think carefully about what they are doing. Sagarin (1992) states:

> The carving process, almost painful for some students during which one must be conscious of every move, every stroke, helps students become conscious of the effects of their labor. We strive for self-consciousness, not in the sense of stage-fright, for example, but for a healthy sense of self in relation to the world. (23)

In grade 10, Sagarin teaches the students Roman calligraphy. He finds that calligraphy is humbling, yet also provides a sense of accomplishment. Sagarin starts by teaching students the appropriate posture and the way to hold the pen. He finds that some students take to the calligraphy easily, while others struggle to get an even flow of ink onto the page. Sagarin (1992) believes that "because of the subtle and precise gestures necessary to draw letters well, perceptual problems often manifest themselves here, and I believe the practice of calligraphy aids development of two-dimensional awareness in ways that the other arts cannot" (23).

In grade 11, the students study medieval romances. One of the art projects that Sagarin has selected as complementary to this study is the construction of stained glass windows. Using Goethe's theory of colours again, students experiment with colour. They also study atmospheric colour in the paintings of Turner, Monet, and others in order to obtain an understanding of general principles of atmospheric colour. In working with glass, differently coloured pieces are interspersed to achieve a blending and balancing of colour. This underscores earlier work with the colour wheel and previous exercises with perception. As colours are blended in the stained glass project, perception of overall atmospheric colour change and the whole effect undergoes a metamorphosis. Students are nearing the end of puberty, so it seems appropriate that one of the themes that is explored during this year is metamorphosis. They are encouraged to look back at who they were and who they might become. Sagarin (1992) comments: "By observing atmospheric color in the stained glass class, they experience a daily and seasonal metamorphosis from which they can learn" (24).

In grade 12, students sculpt life-sized busts in clay. This is similar to work done in grade 8 but now the emphasis is on character rather than caricature. The students can choose from three types of projects: sculpting a bust of a famous person, copying another artist's sculpture, or portraying a particular emotion in the sculpture. Sometimes this sculpture work is done in relation to architecture. This leads to a discussion of how architecture can be an outer expression of inner structures.

Art, then, in Waldorf education allows the students to witness and facilitate their own transformation. Clearly, art, here, is not just self-expression but something that engages the whole student. The intellectual, emotional, and physical faculties are called upon and developed.

Colour is used in so many different ways that students develop a deep sensitivity to beauty.

There are so many stories of how art is being marginalized in public schools with the emphasis instead on language and math. The Waldorf curriculum is a reminder that beauty can still hold a central place in the lives of students.

7

Love as Nonviolence

"It is not a man's duty as a matter of course, to devote himself to the eradication of any, even the most enormous wrong; he may still properly have other concerns to engage him; but it is his duty, at least to wash his hands of it ... If the injustice is part of the necessary friction of the machine of government, let it go ... *but if it is of such nature that it requires you to be the agent of injustice to another, then I say, break the law.*"

– Henry David Thoreau

This quotation changed my life. As a draft-age American in the late 1960s, I struggled with the issue of the Vietnam War and what I would do if called up. After reading about this conflict, I concluded it was a civil war among the Vietnamese people and that American intervention was wrong. If drafted, I would become "an agent of injustice" in an unjust war. So when I was called up, my wife, Jean, and I emigrated to Canada in 1969. This event led me to so many changes in my life, and one was to learn about nonviolence and the work of Martin Luther King Jr. and Mahatma Gandhi.

Mahatma Gandhi devoted his life to the principle of nonviolence, which he equated with love. He considered nonviolence as a science that could be developed through investigation and experimentation. His autobiography was subtitled *The Story of My Experiments with Truth*. Central to his conception of nonviolence was *ahimsa*, or non-harming, which he expressed so beautifully in his book:

> This *ahimsa* is the basis of the search for truth. I am realizing every day that the search is vain unless it is founded on ahimsa as the basis. It is quite proper

to resist and attack a system, but to resist and attack its author is tantamount to resisting and attacking oneself. For we are all tarred with the same brush, and are children of one and the same Creator, and as such the divine powers within us are infinite. To slight a single human being is to slight those divine powers, and thus to harm not only that being but with him the whole world. (Gandhi 2011, 286–7)

Gandhi was influential in the lives of Martin Luther King Jr. and Aung San Suu Kyi and many others devoted to nonviolence. His conception of nonviolence was not a passive one. He used the term *satyagraha*, or "soul force," to describe his understanding of nonviolence. Satyagraha refers to internal strength that carries the person forward; those who practise satyagraha are referred to as satyagrahi. Michael Nagler (2004) has written how problematic it is to associate terms such as "passive resistance" with nonviolence. For Nagler, nonviolence is a "force grounded in nature and exampled in history, is to begin getting our culture back on course" (49).

Gandhi began his practice of nonviolence in South Africa, and his main opponent was General Jan Christian Smuts, head of the British government there. A secretary to Smuts wrote about the power of nonviolence, "I often wish that you took to violence like the English strikers, and then we would know at once how to dispose of you. But you will not injure even the enemy. You desire victory by self-suffering along ... and that is what reduces us to sheer helplessness" (cited in Gandhi 1999, vol. 34, 267). Nagler (2004) writes that nonviolence is a "whole-being experience" that engages the satyagrahi and the opponent. It has the capacity to fundamentally change people and their relationship to one another. It does not just engage the intellect but "heart knowledge" (52). Marshall Frady (1992), writing in *The New Yorker*, describes this kind of power:

[Martin Luther] King started from the essentially religious persuasion that in each human being, black or white, whether deputy sheriff or manual laborer or governor, there exists, however tenuously, a certain natural identification with every other human being; that, in the overarching design of the universe which ultimate connects us all together we tend to feel that what happens to our fellow human beings in some way also happens to us. So that no man can continue to debase or abuse another human being without eventually feeling himself at least some dull answering hurt and stir of shame. Therefore, in the catharsis of a live confrontation with wrong, when an oppressor's violence is met with a forgiving love, he can be vitally touched, and even, at least momentarily reborn as a human being, while the society witnessing such a confrontation will be quickened in conscience toward compassion and justice. (41)

Kenneth Boulding (1989) writes about three conceptions of power. The first is *threat* power, which resorts to threats to achieve its goals, and the second is *exchange* power, in which people agree to make exchanges to reach an agreement. The third is *integrative* power, and nonviolence as cited in the examples above from Smuts and King offers the potential for authentic growth for those involved. Gandhi (1999) wrote, "Power based on love is a thousand times more effective and permanent than one derived from fear of punishment" (vol. 30, 66–7).

Nagler (2004) gives many examples of power of nonviolence in his book. One tells of two women who volunteered to work in El Salvador for Peace Brigades International (PBI). Both were arrested. Marcela Rodriguez was from Colombia and her co-worker, Karen Ridd, was Canadian and was able to contact the Canadian consul and PBI. PBI was able to activate a worldwide network so that people were sending messages to the Canadian and Colombian embassies around the world. After being interrogated for several hours Karen was released, but after walking out of the barracks, she turned around and went back in because she could not walk away from her friend. The guards harassed both of them, but when Karen explained how it felt to be separated from her *compañera*, this somehow resonated with the guards and they let both of them go. Nagler comments, "It's as though her very vulnerability put in her hands some kind of force that worked a minor miracle, even though Karen had not counted on it" (28). The research on nonviolence is just emerging, but Karen's act was one of integrative power. Karen appealed to the human need for connection and fellowship that the guards recognized. Nagler writes this need for connection is a law of nature and that an "act like Karen's has power, because she both opened the soldiers' eyes to Marcela's humanity and offered them an escape from their own hostility" (30). Karen's "courage, her love and her assumption that they (the guards) were human beings capable of humanity were the ingredients of her transformative effect on the men, her magic waking potion" (51).

The media is filled with acts of violence, but we rarely hear about events such as what happened with Karen and Marcela. The journalist Daniel Schorr (1993) wrote, "Television, celebrating violence, promotes violence ... By trivializing great issues, it buries great issues. By blurring the line between fantasy and reality, it crowds out reality" (19).

Historical Examples

Slowly, a science of nonviolence is emerging. This involves examining the many instances where acts of nonviolence were effective either in the short or long term. Mark Kurlansky (2008) has written a history of nonviolence. One of the earliest advocates was the Chinese philosopher Mozi, who wrote about the power of *chien ai*, or mutual love. "Like unto these, too, are state officers and princes who make war on other countries – because they love their own country but no other countries, and so seek to profit their own country at the expense of others. The ultimate cause of all disorders in the world is the lack of mutual love" (cited in Kurlansky 2008, 11).

Kurlansky (2008) writes how Jesus, Buddha, and Mohammed taught about nonviolence or non-harming. In the Sermon on the Mount, Jesus talked about loving your enemy and rejected the use of force. Kurlansky writes that the followers of Jesus, the early Christians, are "the earliest known group that renounced warfare in all its forms and rejected all its institutions" (21). Mohammed endorsed wars of defence but was against wars of aggression. His vision for perfect society in Mecca "enforced a complete ban on violence, which made Mecca prosper as a center of trade" (35). Finally, the Buddha taught that by looking at our minds we gain an awareness that can reduce greed, hatred, and delusion, which are the sources of violence.

The emperor Ashoka, who ruled a good part of what is now northern India from 269 BCE to 232 BCE, adopted nonviolence. Influenced by the teachings of the Buddha, he believed that the *dhamma*, or the order of things, should guide governance. This included acceptance of different religions, helping the poor, and renouncing wars of expansion. He had his edicts engraved on rocks throughout this part of India and many still stand today. The twelfth rock edict focuses on religious tolerance. Bruce Rich (2010), in his book about Ashoka, writes that the emperor believed all religions shared an essential core wisdom that "aims for the good, and that is it his policy to support the progress of all sects because they aim essentially for the same" (119).

Here is the rock edict that mentions the dhamma and the role of meditation:

People can be induced to advance in the Dhamma by only two means, namely moral prescriptions and meditation. Of the two, moral prescriptions are the lesser, meditation the greater. The moral prescriptions I have promulgated include rules making certain animals inviolable, and I have established other rules as well. But even in the case of abstention from injuring and killing creatures; it is by meditation that people have made the greatest progress in the Dhamma. (Cited in Nikam and McKeon 1959, 27–8)

Rich's (2010) book, *To Uphold the World: A Call for a New Global Ethic from Ancient India,* makes a case for how Ashoka's legacy can be influential today. He argues that his greatest legacy was the "practical attempt in the public sphere to introduce (all his flaws not withstanding) a higher ethic of nonviolence and respect for all beings in the practice of politics" (148). There are very few examples in history of how nonviolence has been instituted at a societal level, and thus Ashoka's work deserves consideration and analysis. Rich states that Ashoka "tried to formulate and put into practice a vison of global citizenship, nonviolence – not just toward humans but also toward other sentient beings – responsibility, and justice" (175).

The other example of a societal attempt to institute nonviolence came with William Penn's efforts. William Penn was sent by King Charles II in 1681 to set up a colony in the New World, which later became Pennsylvania. Penn also came with the blessings of his mentor, George Fox, founder of the Society of Friends. Penn governed his territory based on principles of nonviolence and this has been called the "Holy Experiment," which lasted for seventy years. Before Penn came to North America he wrote to the Delaware Natives: "I am very sensible of the unkindness and injustice that hath been too much exercised toward you by the people of these parts of the world ... but ... I have great love and regard toward you, and I desire to win and gain your love and friendship, by a kind, just and peaceable life" (cited in Lynd and Lynd 1995, 2).

Nagler (2004) suggests that despite challenges, the experiment worked "in every department, from defense to criminal justice" (113). It functioned well even though it was surrounded by other colonies and British rule that were based on violence. It included inhabitants from diverse religious perspectives, including not only Quakers but also Mennonites, Dunkers, and the Native population. For the Mennonites, this was the first time that they lived under a government that allowed them to fully participate in the society. The colony did not comply with British conscription and just employed volunteer forces. They adopted their own foreign policy and refused to fight the French or the Aboriginal population, with whom they negotiated friendly relations. They also administered the colony under the "Great Law," where capital crimes were reduced from 200 to two – treason and murder. The Great Law also abolished war. Nagler asserts this law was more progressive than the U.S. crime bill of 1991.

Kurlansky (2008) argues that if the Quakers had controlled the legislature for all of the colonies, the "history of North American, and perhaps, by example, all of the Americas, Africa and much of Asia might have been different" (64). The Quakers believed that non-Christians did not have to be conquered. Eventually, the experiment ended as settlers on the western frontier did not believe in nonviolence and fought with the Natives of that region.

In the twentieth century there have been numerous examples of successful nonviolent activity. Peter Ackerman and Jack Duvall (2000) describe fifteen such events in their book. It is often asserted that nonviolence may have worked in Gandhi's India against the British but could never have been used successfully against the Nazis in Germany. However, there are examples of successful nonviolent actions against the Nazis. One example comes from Denmark. Very early in the occupation, a seventeen-year-old school boy, Arne Sejr, who lived in Slagelse, wrote the Ten Commandments for the Danes. These included:

1 You must not go to work in Germany and Norway.
2 You shall do a bad job for the Germans.
3 You shall work slowly for the Germans.
4 You shall destroy important machines and tools.
5 You shall destroy everything which may be of benefit to the Germans.
6 You shall delay all transport.
7 You shall boycott German and Italian films and papers.
8 You must not shop at Nazis' stores.
9 You shall treat traitors for what they are worth.
10 You shall protect anyone chased by the Germans. (Ackerman and Duvall 2000, 212)

Some of these items, for example, the fourth one, are technically not part of a nonviolent approach. Riding his bike, Sejr delivered his commandments to the mailboxes of Slagelse's most influential citizens. With the help of other high school students, the list was circulated throughout Denmark, and "eventually became sacred to the Danes as they waged their national resistance" (212).

In 1942, two years later, Arne was in Copenhagen having enrolled in the university and, along with other students, was publishing illegal books.

One was the *White Book*, which included documents about the German invasion of Denmark. The government's conciliatory actions described in the book angered many Danes and 20,000 copies were sold.

In 1943, the Germans started to try to round up the Jews. The Danes helped the Jews find places to hide immediately, as Danish institutions protested and the universities in Copenhagen and Aarhus closed for a week in protest. The Danes realized that the Jews needed to be taken out of the country to Sweden. Again, Arne Sejr was involved as he and his fellow students gathered information on the safest escape routes. Five students died in these reconnaissance missions. In total, 7,220 Jews escaped to Sweden.

Another example of successful nonviolence action against the Nazis occurred in Berlin in 1943. The Gestapo began rounding up Jewish men who until then had escaped the Holocaust. When their non-Jewish wives heard about this, they gathered on the Rosenstrasse with goods such as food and clothing for their husbands, whom they believed were being held inside. The crowds grew larger, even though it was very cold. By the end of the second day, 600 women were outside. On the third day, soldiers fired warning shots and the women ran for cover, but later returned. Others joined the protest, so there were about 1,000 protestors on the third day. Finally, the Nazis released the prisoners. Ackerman and Duvall (2000) comment:

> On the Rosenstrasse in 1943, in the center of the century's greatest cyclone of killing, the violence that could have been visited on protesting German women and on almost 2,000 Jews was neutralized – by a few hundred wives who refused to go home. The Nazis' will to violence was notorious. But superiority of military force did not make them invulnerable: they were frightened of protest at the seat of their power, and the potential cost of supressing it with violence – while trifling in blood and time – was politically too high to pay. So the evil they embodied was, in that place and that moment, impotent. (239)

The Rosenstrasse protest was a spontaneous example of nonviolence. Nagler (2004) points out that it lacked what Gandhi and King were able to do and that was follow-up action. Nonviolence is most effective when people are prepared and there is sustained action. Ackerman and Duvall (2000) describe such nonviolent actions from around the world:

- In 1905 the priest Georgii Gapon got 150,000 workers to march in cold weather in St. Petersburg. This led to further protests in Russia and led to the first elected parliament.

- In 1923 German miners and railroad workers protested against French and Belgian soldiers who came to take resources from that region. They did not cooperate and their protests led to Britain and the USA supporting the protest which led to the removal of the soldiers.
- In 1944 in El Salvador, students, doctors, and merchants angry with the repressive activities of the country's dictator were able to get the support of some of the military and others. Without firing a shot, they forced the dictator into exile.
- In the late 1950s and early 1960s Martin Luther King Jr. led the civil rights movement in the southern states in the United States which led to the legislation giving Afro-Americans civil rights and voting rights.
- In the 1970s and 1980s workers in Poland organized and formed Solidarity in that communist country. This is one of the actions that eventually brought an end to communism in Poland and in Eastern Europe.
- In Argentina during the 1980s mothers of missing sons organized protests in central Buenos Aires. Along with the defeat in the Falklands War, these protests led to the downfall of the military dictatorship.
- At the same time, nonviolent protests in Chile forced a plebiscite which led to the removal of General Pinochet.
- In 1986 in the Philippines Ferdinand Marcos was forced to flee the country through protests led by the widow of an assassinated opposition leader.
- In the 1980s and 1990s various groups in South Africa engaged in nonviolent action against apartheid. Along with the sanctions from countries around the world, this activity led to the freeing of Nelson Mandela and the end of the white regime there.
- After the Berlin Wall came down, students in Czechoslovakia sat in Wenceslas Square in Prague chanting, "We have no weapons … The world is watching." The communist regime fell there followed by regimes in Eastern Germany, Hungary, and Bulgaria. (3–4)

Gandhi and the Constructive Program

Nagler (2004) argues that nonviolence is a science that is slowly emerging and that we can study nonviolent events and what is central to their success. Gandhi is perhaps the most famous practitioner of nonviolence. As noted previously, he saw his work as experiments with truth. Most importantly, he believed not just in nonviolent protest but in constructive programs, which involved a comprehensive approach to nonviolence. Although he did not govern India, his approach along with that of William Penn and Ashoka should be considered carefully as we search for a nonviolent future. Nagler argues, "We need a real grasp of the nonviolent principle which will give us an articulate understanding of how to apply it ... and we need some overall design – some coherent, but all-embracing picture – which would help us feel that we're all working together even if we're not working on the same project ... a total nonviolent-guided evolution" (166).

Gandhi was able to launch such a program. He used *charkha*, or the spinning wheel, as the concrete symbol of the program. The charkha could be used to create clothes that were indigenous to India and, combined with not purchasing British clothes, this provided a way that could lead to independence. Gandhi saw the charkha also as way to clothe the poor in India. His program was built on the idea that clothing, food, and shelter need to be provided to everyone. With regard to charkha everyone could be involved in spinning, and he asked people to devote one hour a day to creating cloth. Spinning could be done every day, which would lead to "relentless persistence," which was crucial to any long-term change. The charkha was about self-sufficiency so India could produce the necessary goods it needed without help from England.

Gandhi's focus on food led to his famous protest against the salt tax, captured in the 1982 Attenborough film *Gandhi*. In 1930 the campaign for independence had reached a crucial point as the Indian Congress Party raised the flag of freedom as a signal of a new era in the struggle for independence. India was very tense waiting for either side to make a move. Gandhi was expected to provide leadership, and he withdrew to his ashram to meditate. For weeks he sat quietly while those around him urged him to act and, finally, the answer came to Gandhi in a dream. The British had passed a law which made it illegal for anyone in India to make their own salt. Gandhi saw that this was a perfect example of how the British exploited India, and he felt that the best way to confront the British was to march to the sea and to take some salt from the water there in defiance against the law. This was the famous salt march.

Gandhi started with seventy-eight of his followers and walked twelve miles each day for twenty-four days. Gandhi was sixty-one at the time, yet he walked briskly and energetically for the entire length of the march. When Gandhi reached the water, a huge crowd had gathered to watch him as he took a small bit of salt from the sand. Immediately huge crowds along the coastline gathered salt and then sold it in the cities. As a result, thousands of Indians were arrested and imprisoned, while many others were beaten and killed by the police. Throughout, however, the Indians maintained their peaceful protest. For a long period, Gandhi remained free, but finally the police came and arrested him at his ashram. When he went to prison, there were 60,000 satyagrahi in jail. Gandhi, of course, was imprisoned several times during his life. He used his time there to pray, meditate, read, and answer his mail. Louis Fischer (1954), in his biography of Gandhi, says:

> The salt march and its aftermath did two things: it gave the Indians the conviction that they could lift the foreign yoke from their shoulders; it made the British aware that they were subjugating India. It was inevitable, after 1930, that India would someday refuse to be ruled, and more important, that England would someday refuse to rule.
>
> When the Indians allowed themselves to be beaten with batons and rifle butts and did not cringe, they showed that England was powerless and India invincible. The rest was merely a matter of time. (102)

Nagler (2004) points out that the underlying thread of Gandhi's constructive program was to heal the "brokenness" of Indian society (173). The first plank of the platform was "Communal Unity," which focused on harmony among the groups, including Hindus and Muslims. Second was the Remove of Untouchability. Nagler asserts that the program as a whole was designed to build "loving community" (175). Gandhi believed in "heart unity," which underlies our differences and is part of the human need for well-being. "Heart unity is the basis of loving community. Which means of real community" (175). Nagler writes that there has to be "empathy, which is the means and end of all heart unity techniques" (174). This vision is similar to Martin Luther King Jr.'s idea of "Beloved Community."

Another feature of the constructive program was holistic education. Gandhi (1980) wrote:

> I hold that true education of the intellect can only come through a proper exercise and training of the bodily organs, e.g., hands, feet, eyes, ears, nose, etc. In other words, an intelligent use of the bodily organs in a child provides the best and quickest way of developing his intellect. But unless the development of the mind and body goes hand in hand with a corresponding awakening of the soul, the former alone would prove to be a poor lopsided affair. By spiritual training I mean education of the heart. A proper and all round development of the mind, therefore, can take place only when it

proceeds with the education of the physical and spiritual faculties of the child. They constitute an indivisible whole. According to this theory, therefore, it would be a gross fallacy to suppose that they can be developed piecemeal or independently of one another. (138)

It can be argued that most departments of education have committed the gross fallacy. Gandhi (1980) also wrote, "I would develop in the child his hand, his brain and his soul. The hands have most atrophied, the soul has been altogether ignored" (144). This is even truer now than when Gandhi wrote this. Today, we hear so much about the importance of literacy in language and math to the exclusion of almost everything else in the curriculum. Gandhi wrote, "Literacy is not the end of education or even the beginning ... Literacy itself is no education" (138). He favoured the use of the hands and body in learning, which "imparts ten times as much in this manner as by reading and writing ... An academic grasp without practice behind it is like an embalmed corpse, perhaps lovely to look at but nothing to inspire or ennoble" (139). It can be argued that much education today has become "an embalmed corpse." He felt education should involve "physical drills, handicrafts, drawing, and music ... Music means rhythm, order. Its effect is electrical. It immediately soothes" (143). UN Ambassador Anwarul Chowdhury, in a paper on peace education, wrote, "It is being increasingly realized that over-emphasis on cognitive learning in schools at the cost of developing children's emotional, social, moral and humanistic aspects has been a costly mistake" (Van Hook 2015a, n.p.).

The schools on the Gandhi ashrams reflected these principles. Gandhi called his approach to education *Nai Talim*, which involved teaching principles of nonviolence to children. He wrote, "Our arithmetic, our science, our history will have a nonviolent approach, and the problems in these subjects will be coloured by nonviolence" (Van Hook 2015a, n.p.). While schools under Hitler and Mussolini were focusing on concepts based on violence, Nai Talim helped children resolve problems in life nonviolently. Gandhi (1980) also felt that children should know why they were learning a particular subject or skill. He wrote about children, "We must never put them off. They know more things than we can imagine" (144).

Gandhi shared many of these ideas with Maria Montessori, whom he met in London. She wrote, "[When] we speak of education we are proclaiming a revolution, one in which everything we know today will be transformed. I think of this as the final revolution; not a revolution of violence, still less of bloodshed, but one from which violence is wholly excluded – for the little child's psychic productivity is stricken to death by the barest shadow of violence" (Van Hook 2015b, n.p.).

Education today focuses mostly on getting a job, and Gandhi would have argued that this is not education, which in his view was about the development of the whole person. In the last chapter of this book, we will look at one school that has a holistic focus and, through its connected curriculum, nurtures love and well-being in its students.

The constructive program also included work in other institutions, including hospitals; a total of 1,200 institutions were involved, and most of these still exist today. Nagler (2004) argues that nonviolence is an energy that resides within the human being and it needs to be fostered through such a program. He cites how Martin Luther King Jr. found this energy within himself. In 1955, King received a number of hate-filled phone calls and, one night, there was a call that kept him awake:

> And I got to the point that I couldn't take it any longer. I was weak. Something said to me, you can't call on Daddy now, he's up in Atlanta a hundred and seventy-five miles away. You can't even call on that something in that person that your Daddy used to tell you about, that power that can make a way out of no way.
> … And I bowed down over the cup of coffee. I never will forget it … And it seemed at that moment that I could hear an inner voice saying to me, "Martin Luther, stand up for righteousness. Stand up for justice. Stand up for truth. And lo, I will be with you, even until the end of the world." (Cited in Garrow 1986, 58)

King was listening to the still small voice within. Gandhi said the still small voice within is the ultimate reference point, "I shall lose my usefulness when I stifle the still small voice within" (Van Hook 2015c, n.p.). Before he was killed, King was moving towards trying to develop a comprehensive program that would address poverty as well as the horrors of the Vietnam War. Nagler (2004) argues that the work of King and Gandhi can be continued by each person listening to their "still small voice" within. This is the source of energy that can move the world to a different place. There must be a move away from glorifying war and violence, which permeates news media and entertainment. The challenges here are huge as we have been so conditioned to violence and its place in the world. As Kurlansky (2008) points out, "Just as most news media, political leaders, cultural institutions, and pundits ignore nonviolence and glorify war, the world does not recognize the triumphs of nonviolence" (167). This is where education has a huge role in actually examining the nature of nonviolence and how it can work. One aspect would be to look to people who cultivate "the arts of love," such as King, Gandhi, and Mother Teresa (Nagler 2004, 201).

Nagler (2004) summarizes the importance of the constructive program for Gandhi: "His trust for the future lay mostly in steady, constructive work – steady rather than occasional, work rather than protest, self-uplifting rather than obstructing others, practical and concrete rather than symbolic" (175). Nagler argues that we need to develop our own program today. "The value in such an approach is its vision and its comprehensiveness: the way it addressed every hurting problem with one inspired energy" (175).

Nonviolence: An Alternative to War

To put it simply, war is about killing people. Yet there is evidence that human beings naturally do not want to kill others. Kurlansky (2008) cites the work of Samuel Marshall, also known as "Slam," who wrote a book after the Second World War about how at best only one in four U.S. combat soldiers ever fired their guns and "in most combat units only 15 per cent of available fire power was used" (180). Published in 1947, *Men Against Fire: The Problem of Battle Command* angered the military establishment. Kurlansky (2008) notes that almost all soldiers returning from war do not want to talk about their experiences. Today, we are more aware of just how extensively returning soldiers suffer from post-traumatic stress disorder (PTSD), which is a direct result of war.

In contrast, there have been "armies of peace" that include men and women trained in nonviolence. Gandhi (1999) wrote:

> The Congress should be able to put forth a nonviolent army of volunteers numbering not a few thousands but lakhs [tens of thousands] who would be equal to every occasion where the police and military are required ... They would be constantly engaged in constructive activities that make riots impossible ... Such an army should be ready to cope with any emergency, and in order to still the fury of mobs should risk their lives in numbers sufficient for the purpose ... Surely a few hundred young men and women giving themselves deliberately to mob fury will be any day a cheaper and braver method of dealing with such madness than the display and use of the police and the military. (vol. 73, 2425)

Gandhi proposed the idea of a nonviolent army for India in the Second World War, but because he was imprisoned, he was not able to follow through on this idea. However, one of his closest disciples, Khan Abdul Ghaffar Khan, was able to enact this vision; he was able to do this with the traditional warlike Pathans. Known as Badshah Khan, he was the physical opposite of Gandhi; he was a huge man with big shoulders and dwarfed Gandhi when they stood together. He expressed his concept of Islam in these words: "The Holy Prophet Mohammed came into this world and taught us that man is a Muslim who never hurts anyone by word or deed, but who works for the benefit and happiness of God's creatures. Belief in God is to love one's fellow man" (cited in Kurlansky 2008, 150).

Under Khan's leadership, 100,000 Pathan fighters, all Muslims, formed a nonviolent army that resisted the British without weapons. They were called the Khudai Khidmatgars, the Servants of God. The Pathans had fought in wars for centuries in the Northwest Frontier Province in India. They dispel the myth that nonviolence is only for the gentle. An example of their resistance to the British came when Khan was arrested. The men and women stood their ground as the British attacked. As they were killed, others stood waiting to pick up the wounded and dead:

> When those in front fell down wounded by the shots, those behind came forward with their breasts bared and exposed themselves to fire so much so that some people got as many as 21 bullet wounds in their bodies, and all the people stood their ground without getting into a panic. A young Sikh boy came and stood in front of a soldier and asked him to fire at him which the soldier unhesitatingly did killing him ... The state of things continued from 11 till 5 o'clock. (Easwaran 1999, 123)

However, in another incident, an Indian regiment, the Garhwal Rifles, refused to fire against the Pathans and every soldier was sentenced to a heavy prison term for not shooting.

Civilian-based defence (CBD) is another form of nonviolence. It was employed by the citizens of Czechoslovakia after the Russian invasion of 1968. It included three components. First, there was no physical resistance to the invasion. Second, everyone – men, women, and children – participated. Third, the occupiers were not seen as objects but as human beings (Nagler 2004, 235). CBD was practised for eight months in Czechoslovakia. The Czechs supported one another in a myriad of ways; for example, "alternative universities" were set up. Mikhail Gorbachev was part of a

Russian delegation that went to that country in 1969 to try to win over the youth. He was stunned by the negative feelings towards the Russians, and he returned to Russian realizing the invasion was a failure. This experience influenced his leadership of the Soviet Union, which eventually led to its demise. Václav Havel was part of this resistance, and he argued that people could create a system parallel to the communist institutions. He said as much as possible people should "live within the truth" (cited in Kurlansky 2008, 173).

Search for a Nonviolent Future

At the end of his book, Nagler (2004) identifies the three basic principles of nonviolence and five things individuals can do to make nonviolence a reality. The three principles are:

(1) A seamless nonviolent ethic towards all life and a nonviolent praxis for every life-threatening problem.
(2) The means and ends are indivisible. There is no acceptable form of violent activity.
(3) Nonviolence is a science that will continue to unfold as we examine its various forms. (283)

For each of us, Nagler (2004) suggests the following steps (slightly adapted here):

(1) Avoid the mass media as a source of news.
(2) Take care of yourself spiritually, and include meditation practice. Meditation, along with practices like yoga and qigong, provides a way to genuine health and well-being which are so important in being a satyagrahi. (Meditation will be discussed more fully in the next chapter.)
(3) Adopt an attitude of metta, or friendliness. (This was discussed in the second chapter.) Nagler (2004) cites an activist friend who said "nonviolence is when you 'humanize' your enemy and let your 'enemy' humanize you" (273).
(4) Learn and share the basics of nonviolence – its history, its logic, and its promise.
(5) Look for positive alternatives to violence that are not symbolic but substantive and long term.

Applications to Education

Each of these five steps can be applied to education. The fourth step needs to be included in the history curriculum, which traditionally has focused on wars and leaders. There should be a place in the curriculum where historical examples of nonviolence are presented and discussed along with learning about the many individuals who have practised nonviolence. These individuals include Gandhi and Martin Luther King Jr. as well as less well known individuals such as David Dellinger (1993), who wrote a moving account of his life in *Yale to Jail: The Life of a Moral Dissenter*. Dellinger lived a life of metta and always extended a hand of friendship to others, even to those he strongly disagreed with. Metta, which was discussed in the second chapter, can again be looked at as a way of seeing and interacting with others.

Another focus can be analysing media and film and how violence is featured so frequently. All of Nagler's (2004) suggestions can provide grounds for discussion in classrooms. It is important to approach these discussions as inquiry, where the ideas are explored rather than imposed.

I would like to end this chapter with another example of nonviolence. Bayard Rustin was involved in both the peace movement and civil rights movement in the United States. In 1951, he marched against the Korean War and was attacked with a stick by an angry spectator. Rustin gave him another stick and asked him if he wanted to use both on him. The attacker then threw down both sticks (Kurlansky 2008, 154). The history of nonviolence is filled with such examples that are rarely reported in the media but form a broad and inspiring picture that we need to include in our education. They could inspire us to move forward to a much more peaceful existence.

8
The Gift of Presence

"I believe that presence is equivalent to love. Giving full presence to another is, I believe, the greatest gift a person can offer."

– Avraham Cohen

Presence is an elusive quality but we know it when we encounter it in another person who listens with their whole being. Genuine presence has a healing quality. Presence is critically important in teaching; the teacher who is able to be present to students creates an environment where real learning can occur. When we reflect on teachers who made a difference in our lives, it is often their presence rather than their pedagogy that made that difference.

Debbie Hall (2007), a psychologist, gives a beautiful description of presence.

I BELIEVE IN THE POWER OF PRESENCE

I was recently reminded of this belief when I and several other Red Cross volunteers met a group of evacuees from Hurricane Katrina. We were there, as mental health professionals, to offer "psychological first aid." Despite all the training in how to "debrief," to educate about stress reactions, and to screen for those needing therapy, I was struck again by the simple healing power of presence. Even as we walked in the gate to the shelter, we were greeted with a burst of gratitude from the first person we encountered. I felt appreciated, but somewhat guilty, because I hadn't really done anything yet.

Presence is a noun, not a verb; it is a state of being, not doing. States of being are not highly valued in a culture that places a high priority on doing.

Yet, true presence or "being with" another person carries with it a silent power – to bear witness to a passage, to help one carry an emotional burden, or to begin a healing process. In it, there is an intimate connection with another that is perhaps too seldom felt in a society that strives for ever-faster "connectivity."

... With therapy clients, I am still pulled by the need to do more than be, yet repeatedly struck by the healing power of connection created by being fully there in the quiet understanding of another. I believe in the power of presence, and it is not only something we give to others. It always changes me – and always for the better. (100–2)

It is this "quiet understanding" that can make the difference in teaching. If the student senses our efforts to develop this understanding, then an authentic connection is made. Eckhart Tolle (2005) writes about presence in *The New Earth*. He says that "alert attention is presence ... Being present is always infinitely more powerful than anything one could say or do, although sometimes being present can give rise to words or actions" (84, 176).

The great teachers talked about the importance of presence. There is a story of one of Buddha's followers, who came back to the Buddha and said he forgot to relate the significant teachings in his talk. The Buddha responded that there was no need to worry because his presence was enough. Stephen Mitchell (1991) in his introduction to his translation of the gospels writes, "Like all the great spiritual Masters, Jesus taught one thing only: presence ... He has no ideas to teach, only presence. He has no doctrines to give, only the gift of his own freedom" (10, 16). Mitchell is referring to the inner freedom of living in the now, the eternal now.

The Zen Roshi Shunryu Suzuki tells a wonderful story about the presence of a teacher. He was the head of a temple in Japan and was looking for a kindergarten teacher for the temple school. He identified a woman in the community whom he believed would be a good teacher and repeatedly tried to convince her to take the job, but she refused. Finally, he said to her, "You don't have to do anything, just stand there." When he said that, she accepted the position. He was convinced that her presence alone would make a difference in the lives of the children (Chadwick 1999, 128).

Most of us have had the privilege of having one teacher in our life that was truly present. John Makransky (2007), a Buddhist scholar, describes the presence of one of his teachers, Geshe Tsering:

While studying and engaging in philosophical debates with him, he treated me with such gentle respect and love that, when I reluctantly left at the end of the day, I felt like a different person. Something was awakened in me by his presence, a deep desire to be like him and a recognition that somehow, mysteriously, I could. It made me grateful to be alive. (147)

Makransky (2007) says the teachings flowed from "his whole manner of being. He was a remarkable teacher, whose effectiveness flowed from his unwavering and unconditional love for all whom he served" (147). Makransky's experience supports Avraham Cohen's (2015) assertion that being present is an act of love.

Makransky (2007) suggests teachers meditate in the morning in the following manner:

> … envision yourself receiving the radiance of loving compassion and letting it radiate through you to all your students. Then merge with that radiance and rest in natural awareness. Throughout your day periodically return to this practice and inhabit it. The moment you step into the classroom, begin communing with your students heart-to-heart in pure perception, radiating unconditional care below the radar of self-concerned judgments – theirs or yours. Let your wish for your students' deep well-being help evoke their innate abilities for discernment, compassion, and joy. (208)

Rachel Kessler (2009) also found daily meditation practice "essential to cultivating presence" (21). She would do this practice at home and also take a few minutes before class to centre herself: "I imagine the class I am about to work with. I see myself looking into each pair of eyes, imagining my heart opening to each child" (21). In her work with teachers, Kessler found that "running, hiking, playing a musical instrument, painting, meditation, writing poetry and keeping a daily journal" helped them be more present.

For Kessler (2000) being fully alive is crucial to presence. This involves being:

- Open to perceiving what is happening right now.
- Responsive to the needs of this moment.
- Flexible enough to shift gears.
- Prepared with the repertoire, creativity and imagination to invent a new approach in the moment.
- Humble and honest enough to simply purse and acknowledge if a new approach has not yet arrived. (9)

Presence, then, involves openness and being in the moment so one can respond to what is happening in the classroom.

Catherine McTamaney, in reflecting on her first year of teaching high school, wrote, "I have lost and found hope, reviewed and revised, and finally concluded that my presence here is much more important than I had thought it would be" (cited in Howe 2003, 72). Catherine's insight into the importance of presence is fundamental to making a difference with students.

In my classes I have had many students bring mindful presence into their teaching. A student in my class who teaches in elementary school, Rebecca Ross-Zainotz (2012), worked on being more present to a very difficult student in her class. This boy was constantly seeking attention through negative behaviour towards other students. The student's behaviour was beginning to affect the whole class and the teacher's well-being. So Rebecca decided to be more present to the student. In her own words:

> I decided that in any interaction I had with the student, I would strive to be mindful. I made sure that I was aware and present when I was speaking with him. My body language was attentive and understanding. I made sure that when I was working with him and helping him one-on-one, I made eye-contact and was focusing intently on listening to what he was saying. As he was writing a story about how an animal adapts to its habitat, I could tell he was appreciative of the change; the full attention that I was giving him at that moment. I continued with this approach in my interactions with him. When he would approach with me with a question, or he would raise his hand on the carpet (without interrupting others), I made sure that I was present and aware of him and his request or response at that point in time.
>
> I gave him lots of opportunities to get my positive attention. I wanted him to realize that, when he was doing something positive, he got my positive energy and he got my attention more efficiently and consistently. I wanted him to want to do things that would catch my attention positively so that he would move away from any negative attention that he also may have wanted from me. Every opportunity in which he did something positive, or he was showing a positive attitude, I made sure to, in my mind, think: "I am present in this moment," and acknowledge this. Whether it was him getting out a pencil to complete a task, coming to the carpet on-time, or raising his hand before speaking, I was there, I was present and I made sure that I acknowledged this effort from him. (5–6)

When the student showed negative behaviour, Rebecca tried to not let these behaviours affect her approach:

> There were times, where I had to talk myself through the exercise, and breathe, in order to make sure my mood was not affected, or take a movement break, and speak to another student, but I made sure to focus on being aware of how his behavior was affecting me, and I did my best to not let the negative energy become dominant in me. In these situations, I was very mindful of the words that I used around him, ensuring that they were always positive, and that I would not engage in a power struggle with him. (6–7)

Rebecca felt the whole experience of bringing mindfulness into her teaching was "powerful and moving." She found the behaviour of the student became more positive:

> He seemed to be more understanding of situations where I was helping other students, and not just him (as he would often previously get very upset if I wasn't giving him all my attention). We have now developed a relationship where he knows he will get quality, focused time in which I will help him. I became more consistent with my attentiveness toward him, dealt with him in a mindful manner and his behaviour adjusted.
>
> There are always going to be hard days, and days in which it is hard for him to move past his negative feelings about an issue at school, but on the whole, I feel like he trusts in the fact that I will give him the full attention and positive energy he deserves each day and that this will allow him to be successful. (Personal communication, 2012)

Rebecca also found that benefits of mindfulness impacted her life beyond the classroom:

> I realized that, personally, I have the ability to "take in" and embrace the world around me without "rushing through it," and that interactions with people, especially, those that need us the most, are extremely important to be present in – strangely and unexpectedly, more important for them, than even for us. (Ross-Zainotz 2012, 7–8)

We should not expect a specific outcome from being present. Although we can hope that presence can improve a relationship, the focus should be on simply being there without expectations.

Contemplation and Mindfulness: Ways of Being Present

There are various ways to develop presence; one time-honoured way is through contemplation. Contemplation is a way of knowing when we behold something. The gap between the knower and object of knowing tends to disappear as we can *become* the object that we are observing. Emerson (2003) wrote that the painter painting the tree becomes the tree. This beholding sometimes leads to awe and wonder. Jacques Lusseryan (1987) gives a wonderful example of contemplation. He became blind as a young child but he could still "see" in a contemplative manner:

> Being blind I thought I should have to go out to meet things, but I found that they came to meet me instead. I have never had to go more than halfway, and the universe became the accomplice of all my wishes.
>
> If my fingers pressed the roundness of an apple, each one with a different weight, very soon I could not tell whether it was the apple or my fingers which were heavy. I didn't even know whether I was touching it or it was touching me. As I became part of the apple, the apple became part of me. And that was how I came to understand the existence of things …
>
> Touching the tomatoes in the garden, and really touching them, touching the walls of the house, the materials of the curtains or a clod of earth is surely seeing them as fully as eyes can see. But it is more than seeing them, it is tuning in on them and allowing the current they hold to connect with one's own, like electricity. To put it differently, this means an end of living in front of things and beginning of living with them. Never mind if the word sounds shocking, for this is love. (27–8)

Contemplation, then, can be an act of love. It is a way of being in the world where "we live with things"; there is no "them" but only "us."

Mindfulness

Mindfulness is a form of contemplation. Mindfulness means being totally present in the moment. There are two basic approaches to mindfulness practice. One is a form of meditation where we are present as much as possible to what is happening in the moment with regards to thoughts, feelings, sounds, and body sensations. This is usually done sitting still. Another form is applying attention to our everyday life and involves bringing awareness to our daily activities.

Neither approach is easy. The rush and noise of our world makes it difficult to be fully present. For example, we may try to relax by going for a walk; but we often take our problems with us on the walk. We can take with us a problem from work or our concern over how to pay our bills, and we may find that by the end of our walk we are so preoccupied that we lost our basic awareness of where we were and what we were doing. We didn't really feel the air on our face, or look at the trees, or feel the warmth of the sun.

Another word for mindfulness is wholeheartedness. When you do something you enter into it completely with your whole being, including the body. The whole experience of preparing a meal, eating, and doing the dishes can be done mindfully. For example, as you cut the celery for the salad, you are not preoccupied with thoughts but are just present to the celery. As you eat the meal, you can also focus attention on the eating, chewing, and swallowing. Finally, when doing the dishes, focus on the task. You feel the water as it cascades over your hands and the dishes. Instead of being present, it is easy to be on automatic pilot and not be present in the moment.

One of the first persons to introduce mindfulness in North America was Thich Nhat Hanh (1976) through his book, *Miracle of Mindfulness*. Mindfulness is central to Buddhism. Here is one exercise recommended by Hanh:

Slow-Motion Bath

Allow yourself 30 to 45 minutes to take a bath. Don't hurry for even one second. From the moment you prepare the bath water to the moment you put on clean clothes, let every motion be light and slow. Be attentive of every movement. Place your attention to every part of your body, without discrimination or fear. Be mindful of each stream of water on your body. By the time you've finished, your mind should feel as peaceful and light as your body. Follow your breath. Think of yourself as being in a clean and fragrant lotus pond in the summer. (86–7)

There are similar mindfulness exercises from other spiritual traditions. Consider what the Christian Monks of New Skete (1999) say:

The way we work can change our state of mind. If we clean house conscientiously, even lovingly, our spiritual intentions become evident and are reinforced, and anxieties and petty concerns are put in perspective … Don't fight the task; just carefully and calmly do good work, simply because the house needs to be clean. When your attention strays, focus again on the task at hand, for the quality of your work is also slipping. This exercise results in the satisfaction of having an orderly and clean house, and though you may be tired, you might even feel psychologically refreshed. In the very doing of this, you will experience how even this facet of life is worthy of respect. When you apply this to whatever your life asks of you, your attitude toward everything is transformed. (274–5)

Mindfulness and contemplation are different from *reflection* (Schon 1983*)*. They do not ask the teacher to reflect on something but simply be with the object. Teaching can move back and forth between mindfulness and reflection. Reflection allows us to step back to analyse what we have been doing; mindfulness and contemplation just let us be in the present moment. One way of looking at teaching is the movement back and forth between mindfulness and reflection. Both are essential to good teaching.

Mindfulness in Med

Mindfulness has reached the mainstream. A February 23, 2014, issue of *Time* magazine featured a cover story on mindfulness. Jon Kabat-Zinn (1990) has been a leader in the research on mindfulness. For years he has worked with patients who had reached the end of the line with regard to how conventional medicine could help them deal with problems such as chronic pain. He found that using mindfulness practices led to significant improvement in dealing with these difficulties. Trained as a molecular biologist and working at the University of Massachusetts Medical Center in Worcester, he saw the potential of mindfulness practice for patients at the clinic. Kabat-Zin developed the mindfulness-based stress reduction (MBSR) program for patients, which he ran in the basement of the centre. The program consisted of a one-day session and weekly two-hour sessions, conducted over eight weeks. In 1990, his book, *Full Catastrophe Living,* reported on his program and some of the early research showing the positive effects of the program. Three years later, Bill Moyers, on his PBS program *Healing the Min*d, interviewed Kabat-Zinn and that was when his work became widely recognized. Barry Boyce (2011) writes, "This was the beginning of what we now can call the 'mindfulness revolution'" (xiii).

MBSR is based on the assumption that people can do a lot to aid in their own healing. In an interview with me, Kabat-Zinn said, "Although we can influence healing in many ways, the ultimate capacity for healing lies

within the person" (Miller 1988, 38). Kabat-Zinn talked about how mindfulness meditation is healing:

> One of the consequences of mindfulness meditation is a profound sense of
> relaxation. Another consequence is the falling away of personalized clinging
> and attachment. People see into the deeper aspects of their being and, of
> course, this can be very liberating. Even if people have the smallest taste of
> this experience it usually motivates them to go much deeper into the practice
> … they usually gain something important: self-understanding and acceptance,
> which are fundamental to healing. (40)

Kabat-Zinn has detached MBSR from its Buddhist roots so that the
language is accessible to everyone. He says, "Instead of talking about
wisdom, generosity, attachment, and non-attachment, we talk about self-
confidence, self-esteem, and understanding one's relationship to thought,
reactivity to stressful situations, how reactivity and unmindful thought
can make us anxious" (cited in Miller 1988, 41).

There have been studies conducted on the impact of MBSR. Daniel
Siegel (2011) summarizes some of this research. First, MBSR training
enhances left frontal activity in the brain, which apparently aids people
in "moving towards, rather than away from a challenging external situation." It supports what is called an "approach state" that can be seen "as
the neural basis of resilience" (138). Second, this change in the brain is
also associated with an improvement in the immune system and the ability
to fight infection. Third, the research on MBSR shows that "patients feel
an internal sense of stability and clarity" (138–9). This helps adults and
adolescents with attention difficulties to improve their ability to sustain
concentration. In this regard, MBSR was found to be even more effective than medications. Fourth, MBSR has helped in dealing with a number
of mental health difficulties, including "obsessive-compulsive disorder,
borderline personality disorder, drug addiction and in the prevention of
chronically relapsing depression" (139). Mindfulness meditation helps the
person discern different thoughts and this is a crucial step in "disentan-
gling the mind from ruminative thoughts, repetitive emotions, and impul-
sive and addictive behaviors" (139).

The MBSR program has now spread around the world and is given a
variety of settings. Boyce (2011) writes that these variations include "Mindfulness-Based Childbirth and Parenting, Mindfulness-Based Cognitive
Therapy, Mindfulness-Based Eating Awareness Training, and Mindfulness-
Based Art Training for Cancer Patients" (xiii). Other mindfulness-based

programs include the Mindfulness Awareness Research Center (MARC) at the University of California, Los Angeles (UCLA). Susan Smalley and Diana Winston (2010), who work there, have written in my view one of the best books on mindfulness, *Fully Present: The Science, Art and Practice of Mindfulness.*

Another interesting example of the use of mindfulness comes from the sports arena, and is the work of Phil Jackson, former coach of the Chicago Bulls and the Los Angeles Lakers. In his book *Sacred Hoops,* Jackson (1995) writes:

> When players practice what is known as *mindfulness* – simply paying to what's happening – not only do they play better and win more, they also become more attuned with each other. And the joy they experience working in harmony is a powerful motivating force that comes from deep within, not from some frenzied coach pacing along the sidelines, shouting obscenities in the air. (5–6)

Jackson (1995) also found that when he used mindfulness to listen to his players, he was able to connect with them. He would try to listen without judgment or with what he called an "impartial, open awareness" (67). By simply being present in this way, he felt he got better results than shouting at them or imposing his own agenda. Jackson led his teams to eight NBA championships in a highly competitive environment.

So there is some empirical evidence about the effects of mindfulness practice in different areas of life. Now I would like to turn to education, my own field.

Why Contemplation and Mindfulness in the Curriculum?

One important reason for including contemplative practices such as mindfulness in teacher education is that it can be a form of self-learning. For example, mindfulness meditation is based on the notion that we can learn and grow by simply watching our own experience. As we notice our own thoughts and agendas, we can gain deeper insight into ourselves and the nature of experience. In this context, mindfulness is a *form of inquiry.* In contrast, the model for much learning at the university level is that the professor and the text are the authority and the student must learn from these authorities. Mindfulness meditation provides one alternative to this model and instead recognizes that we can learn from ourselves and our own experience.

Another reason for engaging in contemplation is that it allows teachers to deal with the stresses in their lives. Research indicates that meditation is an effective tool in enhancing physical and mental well-being (Smalley and Winston 2010; Davidson with Begley 2012) and, given the pressures that teachers face today, this aspect of meditation should not be overlooked. The majority of students in my classes have seen the positive effects of contemplative practice in simply being able to address stressful events that come up in their lives. Teachers in my classes comment how they are less reactive to difficult classroom situations. One teacher stated: "I interact with others more calmly, more gently, more compassionately." She works with kids that have behavioural difficulties who are often angry and she said: "I feel a patience with them and tenderness towards them … The kid is being rude – driving me crazy. Instead, I see the kid is hurting and I care for him differently. I think I see the student as myself."

Mindfulness can be important to how we approach teaching. If teaching is ego-based it can become a frustrating series of mini-battles with students. The classroom becomes focused around the issue of control. If we teach from a different place (e.g., heart, soul), teaching becomes a fulfilling and enriching experience. Robert Griffin (1977) summarizes this very well:

> You do not feel set off against them [the students] or competitive with them. You see yourself in students and them in you. You move easily, are more relaxed, and seem less threatening to students. You are less compulsive, less rigid in your thoughts and actions. You are not so tense. You do not seem to be in a grim win-or-lose contest when teaching. (79)

When we teach mostly from our egos, our work can become tense and frustrating. Conversely, when we teach with soul, our work can become an act of joy and delight. Teaching from this deeper place, we experience connections with our students and our colleagues.

My final argument for including contemplation and mindfulness in the curriculum is that these practices offer an opportunity to make our education truly holistic. By holistic I am referring to educating the whole person and not just the intellect. We give lip service to educating the whole human being, however, much of our education system is limited to head learning. One could argue that even this form of learning is very limited and in many cases our elementary schools focus only on the development of a few basic skills and factual recall. This approach to learning is driven primarily by an economic agenda. We hear the mantra constantly that students need to be trained so that they can compete and participate in the global economy. This narrow vision of education has played a role in the corporate corruption that we see today. With the emphasis on individual achievement and test scores our system is basically one of student competition. Our students today are rarely given the larger vision of what it means to be human beings inhabiting the earth and the cosmos.

This was not always the case. Pierre Hadot, the French philosopher, makes the case that ancient philosophy was not just an intellectual exercise but was primarily a contemplative practice. Hadot (2002) states: "To live in a philosophical way meant, above all, to turn toward intellectual and spiritual life, carrying out a conversion which involved "the whole soul" – which is to say the whole of moral life" (65). Philosophy, then, could be called an education of the soul. Hadot describes various spiritual exercises that Greek philosophers pursued in their work as they practiced various forms of contemplation such as being fully present in the moment. For example, the Roman poet and philosopher Horace wrote: "Let the soul be happy in the present, and refuse to worry about what will come later ... Think about arranging the present as best you can, with serene mind. All else is carried away as by a river" (cited in Hadot 2002, 196).

Being in the present requires constant attention. This constant awareness was particularly stressed by the Stoics. Hadot (2002) notes:

> For them, philosophy was a unique act which had to be practiced at each instant, with constantly renewed attention (*proshoke*) to oneself and to the present moment ... Thanks to this attention, the philosopher is always perfectly aware not only what he is doing, but also of what he is thinking (this is the task of lived logic) and of what he is – in other words, of his place within the cosmos. (138)

Hadot (2002) also makes the connection of Greek philosophy to ancient Asian philosophy. He cites his colleague Solere, who writes that "the ancients were perhaps closer to the Orient than we are" (279).

I believe that the Greek academy and the ancient Buddhist university of Nalanda can help us find a new vision for the modern university. Nalanda was founded in the fifth century BC in what is now northern India. At one point there were 10,000 students and 1,500 professors there. At Nalanda, meditation was practised along with scholarship as the university contained both libraries and meditation halls. I had the opportunity to visit the ruins of Nalanda in 1993 and you can still see the outline of these halls and the libraries.

Mindfulness in My Teaching

I have been working with contemplative practices in my classes since 1988. My work is with graduate students in education taking courses in holistic education. It is beyond the scope of this chapter to outline in detail a conception of holistic education. I would just note that holistic education is rooted in the ancient vision of wholeness and moving towards an education that both recognizes and facilitates connectedness (Miller 2007, 2010). I introduce students to mindfulness in both sitting practice and daily activity. With regard to sitting meditation, I introduce students to seven different types of meditation and give them the choice of which one they pursue during the course. Students are encouraged to let go of the *calculating mind* and open to the *listening mind* that tends to be characterized by a *relaxed alertness*.

To date, over 2,000 students have been introduced to meditation practice in these courses. Only four students in twenty-eight years have asked not to do the assignment. So far there has not been one student who has reported an overall negative experience with the practice during the course. Most of the students are women (80 per cent) in their late 20s, 30s, or 40s. Students are asked to meditate each day for six weeks. In the beginning they meditate for about 10 to 15 minutes a day, and by the end of the six weeks they are encouraged to meditate for 20 to 30 minutes. Students are required to keep a journal to reflect on how the process of meditation is going (e.g., how the concentration and focus are going, how the body is feeling, etc.). The journals also focus on how meditation has affected them. Some of the themes students explore in their journals have included the following:

(1) Giving themselves permission to be alone and enjoy their own company
(2) Increased listening capacities
(3) Feeling increased energy
(4) Being less reactive to situations and generally experiencing greater calm and clarity
(5) Sleeping better

I have conducted two qualitative studies on this work with my students (Miller and Nozawa 2002; Miller and Nozawa 2005; Irwin and Miller 2016). Several students in my class have found mindfulness to be a powerful practice. One student describes her experience with the practice. She first describes how it changed her relationship to her own body:

Meditation slowly started to become calming. Bodily awareness started from extremities like the hands and feet, moving to the head and shoulders. In an earlier journal entry, I remember remarking that I could not feel my torso, much like a void that caused disconnection between body parts. It was only weeks in that I could finally centre myself, grounding my awareness to the abdominal region. By this time, I could feel tension oozing out of my body as soon as I settled down in my usual spot. My body recognized what was going to take place and automatically prepared itself. Despite some unsatisfactory sessions, I found myself enjoying meditation in general.

She also saw an improvement in her sleep, which many other students have also noted. "The first change I noticed concerned my sleeping habits. I had been having difficulty falling and staying asleep for a few months. I turned to natural supplements like melatonin or extremely mild anti-anxiety medication when I felt exhausted. However, since meditating, I have been sleeping much more restfully." This student also felt that the practice helped her deal with stress. She wrote, "I constantly churn my worries, building up stress. I know I do it and I know it is horrible but it is difficult to stop." She found the meditation practice helped her:

Meditation has provided me with new strategies to reduce stress, anxiety, anger, and a sense of helplessness. I am becoming increasingly aware of my body's signals, feeling the burning anxiety in my chest, the taut tension creeping into my shoulders as they occur. This helps me utilize preventive/ coping methods (such as taking deep breaths, counting, or relaxing muscle groups) before the tension becomes an avalanche.

Students in my classes from different backgrounds have found mindfulness practice helpful. Here is the experience of one student, Nadia (pseudonym), a Muslim woman who came from Kuwait. Since she came to Canada, she has taught English classes for people in her community. She uses walking meditation and breathing meditation, and repeats mantras and tries to bring mindfulness into daily life. Much of her practice focuses on mindfulness and she has found it very helpful in practising the piano. Nadia comments:

The mindfulness really helps, because it is simple and can be an integral part of whatever I'm doing, even in cooking. I do the cutting, I focus on the smell of the vegetable, it brings me joy, even when I wash the dishes, it makes me happier when I focus. I drift off, of course, but then I bring myself back. (Miller and Nozawa 2005, 47)

Regarding her personal life, Nadia points out that her family was influenced by her meditation practices as she and her husband have learned the mindfulness together. She said, "My husband was enlightened by many of the things I learned and I passed on to him. He helps me a lot in his own way … we learned the mindfulness together. He easily incorporates it in his daily activity" (Miller and Nozawa 2005, 47). Her husband said that she is changing a lot from how she used to be, as he observed the changes through time. Nadia used to worry a lot and now she is trying to focus on the moment rather than being absent-minded and anxious. When she went back to Kuwait, a few of her family members noted that she seemed more relaxed and happier. She was amazed and wondered how she was different from before:

> It changed my life a lot in many ways from inside. I know I'm less anxious and worried, and whenever I let my mind work in the future or in the past, I get upset again and down, and then I have to bring myself back. When I'm thinking of the past or the future, and they're equally painful … I can simply bring myself to the present with a few breaths, breathing deeply, and then focusing on the moment and just doing it without letting thoughts distract me; that's very helpful for me. (Miller and Nozawa 2005, 47)

Nadia is more mindful now, and finds it easier to be present. She reminds herself whenever her mind drifts off to come back to the present. The more she becomes mindful, the easier it is to include mindfulness in her daily activities. She thinks that it is our nature to be in the moment as young children are naturally mindful. As people get older, they change because of many factors, such as trying to meet the expectations of others. She explains that the element of the practice is simplicity, which we cannot complicate by using a lot of words. The next comment describes that the important lesson is in the experience itself:

> I don't need to even describe it, that's the good part. We understand it and we do it. Quieting the mind, actually, is very important. I don't think we have to, though. It's not, "have to," because that's what brought me to trouble in the first place. The "have to," or "I should do this or that" … If any thought comes in, you don't force it out, you let it smoothly go out. It's not having to or forcing something. (Miller and Nozawa 2005, 47)

Nadia also talks about accepting herself: "It's OK … that's one of the things I'm beginning to tell myself. It's a very powerful thing for me.

When I make a mistake, I am very critical about myself, and this is what I'm changing, and I know it's in the process. I'm telling myself it is OK when I make mistakes" (Miller and Nozawa 2005, 48). Meditation seems to help in the process of accepting herself, which was discussed in the chapter on self-love. Finally, Nadia comments on the relation between her faith and the mindfulness practice:

> In Islam, there are many instructions that Muslims are encouraged to do. For example, when we want to enter a room, it's encouraged to enter with the right foot first, and say a kind of short prayer ... I believe that these little prayers and acts are a way to stay present, to be mindful of what we're doing. So, I think that mindfulness is an integral part of any religion. (Miller and Nozawa 2005, 48)

For Nadia, then, her meditation and mindfulness support her religious practices. As I was finishing the first draft of this book, I received an email from her and she said that learning mindfulness was of one of the most important things she learned in graduate school. She still practises today.

Another of my students, Astrid De Cairos, wrote about how she integrated mindfulness into her day of teaching. I have quoted this before in some of my other books but it deserves to be cited here:

> I began each day marveling at the miracle of life, of falling asleep and awakening to a wondrous world. With this thought, I began my morning rituals. Thinking of my daily routines as rituals actually helped me in attaining a more aware state as I washed my face, took my shower, ate my breakfast and walked (or drove) to work. Upon entering the school, I decided to go to my classroom first. I had previously been going into the office to sign in and say good morning, but this took away from the oneness that I needed in my "mindfulness" training. I ritualized all my tasks – walking up the stairs, putting the key into the classroom door, hanging up my coat etc. It was actually amazing how being mindful of these simple tasks allowed me to begin my day in a calm, clear and less cluttered way. How many times had I come into this room, dumped my coat, hat and mitts on my chair, ran to the photocopy room and back, spent another half hour looking for the photocopying I had laid down somewhere, not to mention the frantic search for mitts when it was time to go out on duty? Instead, I began to become aware of my mornings in the classroom and in turn they became calm and focused.
>
> My most favorite part of this pre-school ritual is writing the schedule on the board. My team teacher had tried to talk me out of this June (she writes

the daily schedule for each day on the sheets of chart paper and laminates them). At the time, I explained to her that writing of the schedule on the board had many different purposes for me. The most important one was that it allowed me to center myself in the classroom. I look back now on how intuitive I had been and I am amazed. Being mindful of this particular ritual has made me fully aware of the "here" during the hectic day. I stand at the front of the room and feel the smooth texture of the chalk in my hands. I think about where I am and I observe my surroundings – the plants, the books, the desks, the children's slippers – I am, for the second time that day, amazed at the miracle of life.

The day begins, I stand outside the classroom fully aware of each individual as they enter the room. I interact with them, I say hello, it feels good. This is new, until now I had never made it to the door when the children entered – I was always too busy! I try to maintain this sense of awareness – aware of my feelings (physical and emotional) and my reactions to the things that are happening "now." Of course, the craziness of the classroom day begins and it becomes more and more difficult to maintain this awareness as the day wears on. However, now instead of working through recess, I take the time to visit with colleagues in the staff room. When I can, I take a walk down to the beach at lunch and look out across the lake, mindful of the beauty of the world around me. When the day ends, I recapture this mindful state and fully participate in the end-of-day ritual with my students. After the children have left, I sweep the floor, being mindful of my movements and the sound of the broom. I often begin by thinking that I am sweeping the day's events away and that I am focusing on the "now" – the actual act of sweeping. The pleasure of being here, and being able to fully participate reminds me again of the miracle of life. (Miller 2006, 79–80)

Mindfulness changed her teaching day and brought her these little "miracles." Astrid brought mindfulness into her teaching as not just a technique but as a *way of being* in the classroom. Her approach can inspire other teachers to develop their own approach as to how they could develop their own presence in the classroom.

9

Eros

In the ancient world, Eros's function as a god was to bring harmony to the universe. Dante also saw love as a divine energy that animates the universe, and he concludes *The Divine Comedy* with the famous lines that it is "Love that moves the Sun and the other stars" (894). Gandhi and King also describe love as the animating force in the universe. Martin Luther King Jr. wrote:

> I have discovered that highest good is love. This principle is at the center of the cosmos. It is the great unifying force of life. When I speak of love, I am speaking of that force which all the great religions have seen as the supreme unifying principle of life. Love is the key that unlocks the door which leads to the ultimate reality. (Cited in Lin 2006, xxii)

Gandhi (1980) wrote, "It is my firm belief that it is love that sustains the earth. There only is life where there is love. Life without love is death. Love is reverse of the coin of which the obverse is truth. It is my firm faith ... that we can conquer the whole world by truth and love" (65). Clarence Darrow, the famous lawyer and an atheist, wrote about the "law of love." He believed that "it is the greatest and most potent force in all this great universe" (cited in Farrell 2012, 276).

Eros is experienced as divine energy that runs through the universe and ourselves. We feel connected to something larger than ourselves.

Sometimes this can happen simply listening to music or walking near the ocean, or it can be an experience of what Richard Bucke (1982) called cosmic consciousness. Bill W., the founder of Alcoholic Anonymous, had such an experience. Robert Thomsen (1975) describes this moment in his biography of Bill:

> ... in that very instant he was aware first of a light, a great white light that filled the room, then he suddenly seemed caught up in a kind of joy, an ecstasy such as he would never find words to describe. It was as though he was standing high on a mountaintop and a strong clear wind below against him, around him, and through him-but it seemed a wind not of air but of spirit-and as this happened he had the feeling that he was stepping into another world, a new world of consciousness, and everywhere there was a wondrous feeling of Presence which all his life he had been seeking. Nowhere had he ever felt so complete, so satisfied, so embraced. (201)

The moment passed, but it was beginning of Bill's path towards recovery and starting AA.

One of the 12 steps is a belief in a higher power, "a power greater than ourselves that could restore us to sanity" (Thomsen 1975, 333). He also felt there was a "mysterious ingredient" in the concept of anonymity that held AA together. At the core it was the experience of one drunk simply talking to another drunk and, for Bill, when this happened, he felt "himself drawing closer to some indefinable force. Then he was truly living in the now ... Conscious simply of the person he was with, he would become aware only of the moment, the immensity and movement of the moment. Sometimes when this happened it was almost as if distant chords of music had begun to sound, but he could never say what struck them" (Thomsen 1975, 298).

Bucke (1982) describes his own experience of cosmic consciousness and what the experience included:

> A sense of exultation, of immense joyousness accompanied or immediately followed by an intellectual illumination quite impossible to describe ... he saw and knew that the Cosmos is not dead matter but a living Presence, that the soul of man is immortal, that the universe is so built and ordered that without any peradventure all things work together for the good of each and all, that the foundation principle of the world is what we call love and that happiness of everyone is in the long run absolutely certain. (8)

In his book, Bucke describes the experiences of several people, including Buddha, Jesus, Plotinus, Mohammed, Dante, Blake, and Walt Whitman.

Near Death Experience and Eros

Some people who have had near death experiences (NDE) also describe the powerful experience of universal, unconditional love. Anita Moorjani (2012) had an NDE when she almost died from cancer:

> In my NDE state, I realized that the entire universe is composed of unconditional love, and I'm an expression of this. Every atom, molecule, quark, and tetraquark is made of love. I can be nothing else, because this is my essence and the nature of the entire universe. Even things that seem negative are all part of the infinite, unconditional spectrum of love. In fact, Universal life-force is love and I'm composed of Universal energy! (139)

People who have experienced NDE find their lives transformed and want to be of service to others. Another example is the work of Eben Alexander (2012), a neurosurgeon. Again the central experience in his NDE was one of love, unconditional love:

> Love is without a doubt, the basis of everything. Not some abstract, hard-to-fathom kind of love but the day-to-day kind that everyone knows – the kind of love we feel when we look at our spouse and our children, or even our animals. In its purest and most powerful form, this love is not jealous or selfish, but unconditional. This is the reality of realities, the incomprehensibly glorious truth of truths that lives and breathes at the core of everything that exists or that ever will exist, and no remotely accurate understanding of who and what we are can be achieved by anyone who does not know it, and embody it in all of their actions. (71)

The work of physician Jeffrey Long is important in the study of NDEs. Long (2010) started the Near Death Experience Research Foundation (NDERF). As part of his research, Long has used a detailed questionnaire to gather information from 1,300 people who have had an NDE. Ninety-five per cent of the respondents felt their experience was "definitely real." Again, Long found that love was central to the experience. He also found a strong consistency among the different people in his research. Long included people from around the world and he found that "our collection of NDEs from cultures worldwide shows striking similarity in content among them all" (50). He also found that "pre-existing cultural beliefs do not significantly influence the content of NDEs" (150). As an example, Long cites the experience of one woman from Colombia. Some of the wisdom she gained from her experience, which is shared by so many others, included:

- We live in a "plural unity" or "oneness." In other words, our reality is "unity in plurality and plurality in unity."
- That I was everything and everything was me, without essential difference other than in earthly appearances.
- That there is no God outside ourselves, but rather, God is in everything and everything is a part of God as is life itself.
- That everything is part of an essential game of life itself, and to that degree we live by true love – unconditional and universal.
- That "I" includes "we."
- That the "creator" is eternally creating, and one of the creations is the practice of conscious love. One learns to paint by painting.
- Consciously living by love is the essence of life itself. (159)

In reflecting on the commonality of NDEs across cultures Long (2010) writes, "It's amazing to think that no matter what country we call home, perhaps our real home is in the wondrous unearthly realms consistently described by NDErs around the world" (171). One could say that our real home is where love and compassion reside.

Long (2010) also writes about how most who have experienced an NDE are transformed by their experience. He found that they "often become more loving in their interactions with others and increasingly value positive and empathic relations" (181). He cites research by Pim van Lommel (2004), who wrote that "love and compassion for oneself, others and for nature" became central to their lives. "They understood the cosmic law that everything one does to others will ultimately be returned to oneself: hatred and violence as well as love and compassion" (118). Long (2010) writes that people who have experienced an NDE tend to inspire love, create empathy, and connect to others in deeper and more fulfilling ways (197). Long also acknowledges how working in this field has "made him a better doctor" as he shows "more love to others" (202).

Eros as Divine Energy

Anne Hillman (2008), writing in the tradition of Teilhard de Chardin, writes about love and the "fire" of transformation:

> The root yearning hidden beneath all human desires is for a Love that has long been calling us. Love's whispered call is not only personal; it breathes through the soul of every human being. We are all being carried on the same tide, drawn by both the call and our yearning as inexorably as the moon draws the movement of the waters. (38)

Teilhard de Chardin believed the universe is headed to the Omega point, a place of divine unification. This is the tide Hillman (2008) is referring to. She writes at the end of her book, "You are part of a great leap of loving such as the world has never known" (347). "There is an Intelligence, a Love within which we are enfolded, a larger Field in which we live" (284). Eros here is a vast energy field of loving presence. This field has also been called the Tao; Jesus called it the Kingdom. Hillman cites D.H. Lawrence (1993) and the need to restore love as central to our existence:

> In every living thing there is a desire for love, for the relationship of unison with the rest of things ... Oh what a catastrophe for man when he cut himself off from the rhythm of the year, for his unison with the sun and the earth. Oh what a catastrophe, what a maiming of love when it was made a personal, merely personal feeling, taken away from the rising and setting of the sun, and cut off from the magical connection of the solstice and equinox. That is what is wrong with us. We are bleeding at the roots. (323)

Hillman (2008) suggests various ways to answer the call to greater love, including meditation, spending time in the wilderness, working with dreams, and learning to listen in a new way. The listening she refers to is listening to the "song of the soul," which may "call you through scripture or poetry. You may find it in art or music, in nature or in the elegance of mathematical equation" (81). Hillman believes connecting with love requires an interior stillness. Here the person goes beneath the surface noise of life and hear the deeper energy that Lawrence refers to.

Hillman (2008) references several people who experienced the fire of love. Teilhard de Chardin had an experience of cosmic consciousness where he experienced "an explosive bliss that was completely and utterly unique" (217). There was also Blaise Pascal who experienced the "night of fire" where he had a direct experience of the divine. Thomas Merton experienced a "spark that was an event, an explosion" (cited in Hillman 2008, 217). Like the experience of the NDE, these "explosions" led to the person being more loving and compassionate. For Hillman (2008), this is the fire of transformation. Tielhard de Chardin believes that "the fire of love may be the only energy capable of extinguishing the threat of another fire, namely that of universal conflagration and destruction" (cited in Hillman 2008, 264).

We can link this love with the nonviolence that Gandhi and King talked about as the way to a world where there would be a Beloved Community, another image of the Omega point.

Science, Math, and Love

Einstein believed there was an underlying harmony to the universe. He spent his life searching for this this unity; he was looking for a unified field theory that would explain this harmony. He did not succeed, but this did not dampen his belief that there was a "harmonious reality underlying the laws of the universe and the goal of science was to discover it" (Isaacson 2007, 3). Einstein wrote, "A spirit in the laws of the universe – a spirit vastly superior to that of man, and one in the face of which we with our modest powers must feel humble. In this way the pursuit of science leads to a religious feeling of a special sort" (cited in Isaacson 2007, 550–1). This reverence and awe were important to how Einstein approached science; he felt this wonder was the true source of art and science. Isaacson (2007), in his biography of Einstein, writes that what made him special was a deep humility that arose from being awed by the beauty of nature. I believe that "mystery" that Einstein refers to is not dissimilar from the idea of the Tao or a hidden reality that underlies the physical universe.

Edward Frenkel (2013), professor of mathematics at the University of California, Berkeley, writes about the beauty and elegance of mathematics and how it reveals a hidden reality at the heart of the universe. He cites Einstein in his book, *Love and Math*. "Everyone who is seriously involved in the pursuit of science becomes convinced that some spirit is manifest in the laws of the Universe – a spirit vastly superior to that of man, and one in the face of which we with our modest powers must feel humble" (241). Like Einstein, Frenkel asserts that there is "something rich and mysterious lurking beneath the surface" and that this hidden reality can be discovered through mathematics. He hopes we can reach a complete understanding of the universe and that such a theory would be "simple and elegant." He adds that "simple and elegant do not mean easy" (201). Frenkel, along with other mathematicians, believes that mathematics inhabits its own world and the work to discover mathematical truth. He writes:

> In my view it is the objectivity of mathematical knowledge that is the source of limitless possibilities. This quality distinguishes mathematics from any other type of human endeavor. I believe that understanding what is behind this quality will shed light on the deepest mysteries of physical reality, consciousness, and interrelations between them. In other words, the closer we are to the Platonic world of math, the more power we will have to understand the world around us and our place in it. (235)

Frenkel (2013) has also made a film about love and mathematics. He does not believe that there is mathematical formula for love but that mathematics "can carry a charge of love" (241). Frenkel believes that the quest to unfold the hidden reality through mathematics is actually a spiritual function. This is not a postmodern vision or a modern view, but an ancient one found in the perennial philosophy which asserts there is an ultimate reality.

He closes his inspiring book with this:

> My dream is that one day we will all awaken to this hidden reality. We may then perhaps be able to set aside our differences and focus on the profound truths that unite us. Then, we will all be like children playing on the seashore marveling at the dazzling beauty and harmony we discover, share and cherish, together. (241)

Closing Note

I have not had an NDE or an experience of cosmic consciousness. In moments of meditation or when listening to the music of Mozart, Schubert, and Haydn, I have felt the "the hidden reality" and the mystery of existence. What are the educational implications of Eros? First, it is possible to experience profound states of consciousness and they should not be dismissed. The media, academia, and our materialist culture tend to deny these experiences; holistic education should help children and adolescents to trust their experience. Also the work of mathematicians like Frenkel need to be included in the curriculum to help students see the beauty of math. Einstein asked the question, Is the universe friendly? and answered in the positive. In a troubled time where our own world can seem hostile, it is important to present a more positive image of the universe that has been shared by scientists and mystics for centuries.

10
Love and Education

"It was great to walk into the school and be respected not just a teacher but as a person. You are honoured and loved. To have your opinion valued. To have the amazing support of administration. Also parents volunteering, giving presentations, giving their time. It is just incredible. One of the things is the community that people have built. So happy to be part of it."

"I come to school every day so fortunate and grateful that I am here. I really love it here. I feel valued and respected by the kids. There is such a love affair. Parents are fantastic, so amazing. Who would not want to come to a place where you are valued? It is absolutely a great fit and I am proud to be here. How you are with kids reflects you wanting to be here."

These are the comments of two teachers who work at a public elementary school in Toronto. I have been connected to this school since its inception and believe it is good example of how love can manifest in a school setting. In this chapter I will write about this school and about my own classroom. It is important also to explore the Shadow of Eros, which Rachael Kessler (2002) did in an important paper. There is also a brief discussion of the Nordic Theory of Love and whether societies and institutions can really provide a basis for a loving society.

Equinox Holistic Alternative School

In 2007 I was approached by a group of parents and teachers who wanted to establish a school in the Toronto school system that would focus on the whole child. Initially, the school was called the Whole Child School and it opened in the fall of 2009. It is now in its ninth year and has been renamed Equinox Holistic Alternative School. The original proposal cited a vision of whole child education from my book *The Holistic Curriculum* (2007):

> We care about children. We care about their academic work. We want them to see the unity of knowledge. We want students to see how subjects relate to one another and to the students themselves. We find that the arts, or more generally an artistic sense, can facilitate connections between subjects.
>
> We care about how children think, and in particular, we try to encourage creative thinking. We want the students to be able to solve problems and use both analytical and intuitive thinking in the process. We care about the physical development of the student. We devote part of the curriculum to activities that foster healthy bodies so they feel "at home" with themselves.
>
> We care about how students relate to others and to the community at large. We focus on communication skills, and as the students develop we encourage them to use these skills in a variety of community settings. We encourage the community to come to the school, particularly artists who can inspire students' aesthetic sense.
>
> Most of all, we care about the students' being. We realize that the final contribution that they make to this planet will be from the deepest part of their being and not just from the skills we teach them.
>
> We can try to foster the spiritual growth of the student by working on ourselves as teachers, parents and community to become more conscious and caring. By working on ourselves, we hope to foster in our students a deep sense of connectedness within themselves and to other beings on this planet. (12)

Whole child education and holistic education are based on the principle of interdependence and connection. In *The Holistic Curriculum*, six connections are presented that formed the framework for the curriculum of Equinox. I conducted a qualitative study of the school, which included interviews with teachers, parents, and students, and some of the comments from teachers, students, and parents are cited here (Miller 2016).

Thinking Connections. This connection focuses on linking the left and right brain. The left brain is seat of logical, sequential, and analytic thought while the right brain is intuitive and holistic. One of the most comprehensive discussions of the two sides of the brain comes from McGilchrist (2009). The first 200 pages of his book examine the research on the brain. He summarizes the differences in this way:

The worlds of the left hemisphere, dependent on denotative language and abstraction, yields clarity and power to manipulate things that are known, fixed, static, isolated, decontextualised, explicit, disembodied, general in nature, but ultimately lifeless. The right hemisphere, by contrast, yields a world of individual, changing, evolving, interconnected, implicit, incarnate, living beings within the context of the lived world, but in the nature of things never full graspable always imperfectly known – and to this world it exists in a relationship of care. (174)

In the rest of the book, McGilchrist (2009) describes how the left hemisphere has come to dominate Western society. He believes the two spheres ideally should be linked as the left hemisphere needs to work within the larger perspective of the right. He argues, "The left hemisphere, isolating itself from the ways of the right hemisphere, has lost access to the world beyond words, the world 'beyond' ourselves" (399).

At Equinox students are encouraged to use both sides of their brain. They learn to think both critically and imaginatively. This is done through the arts, experiences in nature, and an integrated approach to learning where subjects are connected around themes.

Subject Connections. Whole child education attempts to connect and integrate subjects so students can see how knowledge is interconnected and not just limited to separate subjects. One example of this was a project on breeding salmon at Equinox, which was described in chapter 5. Other examples from the school include putting on a play every year, such as *A Midsummer Night's Dream*, and exploring themes and issues that arise from the play.

One of the graduates who is now in high school commented on the impact of the integrated/inquiry-based approach. "They found interesting ways to teach us ... This really got the information into your brain and [it] stay[ed] there, rather than forgetting it in two days. I liked the focus on the arts." This student also commented on the value of the salmon project.

Earth Connections. Students need to see their relationship to the earth and its processes. At Equinox there is a strong emphasis on nature. For example, each day starts with classes going outside and doing various exercises. The children in kindergarten spend most of the day out of doors. For all the classes, there is usually one field trip every week where they visit a nearby ravine or a park that is on Lake Ontario. Throughout their time at the school students keep a nature journal in which they record their observations and reflections on their experiences in nature. One parent commented on how being in nature allowed two different students to bond:

> I saw one boy who was known as bully in his previous school working with a girl. She was an artistic, creative person who had been bullied in her previous school. She was teaching him about knot tying and I saw all those barriers and labels falling away. How would they have interacted in typical classroom setting? It is outside and they feel less exposed. I also saw kids working cooperatively on projects together. It seemed to happen so organically. It was amazing.

Community Connections. Community is crucial to holistic education. Students need to experience community in their classrooms and the school. Teachers, parents, and students experience a strong sense of community at Equinox. The comments by teachers at the beginning of this chapter show this. One parent's comment is representative of other parents' perceptions of community: "I love the community that I feel a part of. People are generous and care about our children." Students also commented on the sense of community.

Community is built through three main factors – rituals and celebrations, circles, and looping. There are many celebrations throughout the year. At the beginning of the year there is an acorn ceremony where each new student receives an acorn and walks under a bridge to celebrate his or her entrance into the school. Classes often meet in circles so students can share their thoughts and feelings, and each day begins with a meeting in a circle outside. Looping involves students staying with the same teacher for more than one year, which allows the students and teacher to bond.

Body/Mind Connections. Holistic education recognizes the relationship between mind and body and helps students see and nurture that connection. For example, mindfulness practices where students witness how breathing can affect one's thoughts are often used to facilitate this connection. At Equinox, mindfulness and meditation are used by most teachers. One teacher, after introducing the students to meditation, has the students lead the practice. This teacher commented that they look forward to the practice and it helps them settle down when they come in from outside. One student who had graduated from Equinox said that learning there "focuses on the whole child. Not just teaching academics. Really teaches the entire body."

Soul Connections. Emerson (1982) wrote that "education is the drawing out of the soul" (80). However, the term soul is rarely heard in educational discourse and is defined here as a vital and mysterious energy that gives meaning and purpose to one's life. Holistic education acknowledges the spiritual life of the student and seeks to nourish the student's soul life. This is done at Equinox through some of the activities already mentioned, including being in nature and exposure to the arts. Teachers and parents commented on how they honour the students and accept them for who they are. One parent with a daughter who graduated commented:

> Another thing is how accepting her generation is of my generation. It is counter to the idea that teenagers hate their parents. Her friends say "hi" to me and hug me. When I would go to the school and half the class would see me and say "Hi, Janet" [pseudonym]. I do not think that behaviour is common. It should be normal but it is not common. I felt honoured to be part of that.

One graduate of Equinox said, "I felt the school helped parents give more respect to kids." From this honouring and respect arose the love that teachers and parents experienced around the school.

With the emphasis today on standardized testing, the focus is on separate subjects rather than on integrated learning. Competition around these tests also separates students from each other. In contrast, education that focuses on connections provides a foundation for love. Relationships are nurtured. If indeed reality at its core is interdependent and connected, then education needs to reflect that reality and not run counter to it.

Nordic Theory of Love

We hear a lot today about Finland's education system as their students score high on the international tests, yet they do not use standardized tests. Recently, the Ministry of Education in Finland announced that it is doing away with subjects at the secondary level and learning will focus on broad "topics" or "phenomena." More and more, Finland is basing its curriculum on the concept of connectedness. In the primary years they do not grade children, as the major focus is on the children's well-being. One of the stated goals of the system is the development of holistic individuals (Sahlberg 2011, 17). Clearly the goal of the system is not just academics but the development of the whole person who sees the interdependence of life.

It is beyond the scope of this book to provide an in-depth description of Finland's education system, but I would like to mention what Anu

Partanen (2016) calls the Nordic Theory of Love. Partanen is Finnish but married to an American and now lives in the United States. In her book she argues that through their institutions, including education, Nordic societies provide a secure foundation so that people can freely develop their own lives. She describes this theory:

> Rather the goal has been to free the individual from all forms of dependency within the family and in civil society: the poor from charity, wives from husbands, adult children from parents, and elderly parents from their children. The express purpose of this freedom is to allow those human relationships to be unencumbered by ulterior motives and needs, and then to be entirely free, completely authentic, and driven purely by love … Liberated from many of the onerous financial and logistical obligations of the old days, we can base our relationship with family, friends, and loved ones more on pure human connection. We are also freer to express our true feelings in our relationship with others. (52–3)

Partanen's experience in the U.S. revealed that life there tends be one of constant anxiety because child care, education, health care, and other aspects of the society are fragmented and do not provide this secure foundation. It is a constant struggle to pay for child care, private schools, and university. A UNICEF study confirms her generalization as it found that countries where children's well-being ranked highest were the Netherlands, Norway, Iceland, Finland, and Sweden. The United States came in thirty-third. Partanen's (2016) book describes in detail the approach to health care, education, child care, and other aspects of life in the Nordic countries and how it allows for "pure human connection."

I am sure many Americans would question her argument, but the success of the Nordic countries in providing such positive conditions for children's well-being needs to be examined and explored further. We need to move away from the Darwinian vision of life that permeates much of life in the United States.

Eros's Shadow

The late Rachael Kessler (2002) wrote a powerful essay entitled "Eros and the Erotic Shadow in Teaching and Learning." I want to include her work here because there is a shadow side to Eros that is rarely addressed. She starts the essay by citing Dan Liston (2000), who discusses love in teaching:

As teachers we share this love of learning with our students. To teach is to publicly share this love; it is to ask others to be drawn in by the same powers that lure and attract us; it is to try to get our students to see the grace and attraction that these "great things" have for us. In teaching we reach out towards our students in an attempt to create connections among them and our subjects. We want them to love what we find so alluring. To love teaching is to be enamored of the attempt to share the attraction and hold the world has on us. To love teaching is to give yourself in a way that can be so tenderly vulnerable. (92)

Kessler (2002) comments, "Without access to Eros, our teaching becomes flat, mechanical, alienating" (268). Yet she acknowledges that when Eros is released there is a "dangerous side" which needs to be acknowledged or it can suddenly arise and create difficulty in the classroom. She writes that as teachers we may feel "romantic love, sexual attraction, even obsession" towards our students. These powerful feelings can carry us away and we can temporarily lose a sense of responsibility. We read in the news of a teacher in high school having an affair with a student. The danger is that we can act on our feelings towards the student or we can repress Eros, where we can "stonewall" a student or let the warmth and energy diminish in the classroom.

Carl Jung introduced the concept of the Shadow, which involves behaviours and feelings that we adopted when we were young to make our way in the world. As we mature we try to disown some of these behaviours – "anger, aggression, greed, or sexual hunger" – and they sink into the Shadow because we felt ashamed about them when we were growing up (Kessler 2002, 270). Kessler (2002) points out that this includes positive behaviours as well as those we may disown. She cites the work of Robert Johnson (1991), "But anything better also goes into the shadow. Some of the pure gold in our personality is relegated to the shadow because it can find no place in the great leveling process that is culture" (8).

Kessler (2002) writes that children and adolescents are sensitive to our unconscious behaviours as teachers. When teachers deny inner feelings connected with the Shadow they can end up acting impulsively or repressing their feelings, leading to a classroom that is arid and mechanical. "The joy and playfulness we dare not express, the sorrow or vulnerability we are afraid to feel – these and other unclaimed dimensions of our wholeness become barriers which limit the freedom of discovery in both teacher and student" (270).

Kessler (2002) provides examples from her own experience of how she dealt with Eros in her teaching. One was where she had some romantic feeling for a secondary school student named Daniel. She recognized her feeling but did not act on it. Instead, she was able to give attention to the student in a loving way. "When I took him aside to talk with him, there was love in my heart. I saw his face soften in a way I had never seen. He looked thoughtful and curious as I spoke to him, telling him what it feels like as a woman to be treated that way. He got it" (278).

Through Daniel she also saw a part of her Shadow. She was living in Los Angeles with all its glitz. Her encounters with Daniel awakened her to her own denial of how she was drawn to the consumerism in LA:

> Listening to Daniel, I suddenly saw that I, like many, had a side of me that was utterly seduced by wealth and fame. Until I arrived in LA, this side had been locked tightly in my Shadow. My presenting self – which I had always believed to be all of me – was the anti-materialist, social activist, service-oriented woman my immigrant family had raised me to be. But surrounded by the glitz of LA, a glamour-lover was desperately trying to get out. As long as I tried to hide from her, she had the power to sneak up on me and run the show. I could not "handle" her until I accepted her – even loved her. And loving Daniel – who was the ultimate expression of this side of my own Shadow – was the way I could accept and bless this very real part of myself. (2002, 279)

In summarizing, Kessler (2002) says the teacher who cannot look at their Shadow "cannot really afford to love, and cannot express the quality of power that ensures safety in a classroom" (283). She argues that teachers need to be "at home in those uneasy domains of our own unconscious" (283). This means being in touch with the "not-beautiful" part of ourselves which then allows us to see the "not-beautiful" in our students with compassion and forgiveness. Kessler cites Johnson (1991) again, who writes, "As the shadow is drawn up into our consciousness, it becomes softer, more pliable, more gentle" (41). In contemplative practices we can begin to witness our Shadow and thus let it come forth in the manner that Johnson and Kessler suggest.

Love asks us to risk and step into the unknown. This fear also needs to be acknowledged as we never know how a relationship will evolve. Will there be rejection or loss? Love requires courage as we enter into any relationship.

My Classroom

As mentioned earlier I teach courses in holistic education, spirituality in education, and contemplative education. Most of these are graduate courses for teachers, although I have also taught a course in holistic education for pre-service teachers. I teach at the University of Toronto; the City of Toronto has been identified as the most multicultural city in the world and my classes reflect that diversity. Of course, most students come from Canada, but other students have come from the following countries: Brazil, Chile, China, Egypt, India, Italy, Japan, Kenya, Korea, Malta, Rumania, Saudi Arabia, Turkey, Ukraine, and Vietnam. My courses are capped at 25 but sometimes they expand to 27 or 28. I find a class in the low 20s allows for the most interaction.

I start my courses by going over the syllabus and then arranging the chairs in a circle, which is the basic structure for the rest of the course. Sitting in a circle goes back to Indigenous peoples and I believe that the circle can provide a healing environment. Emerson (2003) called the circle the "first of all forms" (312). There are no tables or desks, so the class goes "topless" with no computers in front of the students. I suggest that students do not take notes unless someone says something that they really need to write down. All of this is done so students are present to one another. I talk about the importance of presence as key to building community in the classroom, and I also attempt to be present as much as possible during the class.

My pedagogy employs three basic approaches to teaching: transmission, transaction, and transformation (Miller 2007, 2010). *Transmission* is simply conveying information or ideas, usually through a mini-lecture format. *Transaction* involves students interacting with each other, usually in small groups, to discuss ideas that are presented or to address some task or problem. For example, on the first day of my class on the Holistic Curriculum I give students a handout that has six different conceptions of holistic education and ask them to choose one they prefer and then discuss their choice in small groups. *Transformational* approaches attempt to connect to the inner life of the student, and one that I use is the loving-kindness meditation that we do at the beginning of each class. I try to use the three approaches to develop a *rhythm* in my teaching in moving from one approach to the other. Waldorf education uses breathing in and out as a metaphor for teaching and moving between the three approaches allows the classroom to breathe.

Another major component of my courses is that students work in small groups to make presentations to the class. Students bring a wealth of knowledge and experience to the class and this is an opportunity to share that expertise. Each group decides on the topic and format although I ask that the presentations employ the three approaches – transmission, trans-action, and transformation – so that the learning experience is holistic. The groups range in size from two to five students. Students often bond in these groups since they meet together for most of the course. My class-room then has whole group learning in the circle, small group learning in a variety of formats, and individual learning that occurs through the medita-tion. Thus learning is occurring at three different levels. These learnings can come together to make a difference in the lives of the students.

About halfway through my course I share my own journey and how I got involved in holistic education; my story can be found in the appendix to this book. Over the years many students have expressed their apprecia-tion of my effort to do this.

In all my classes I ask students to do some sort of practice. In two classes I ask them to meditate for six weeks, and in the other class I let them select a practice which can also include meditation, keeping a gratitude journal, doing yoga or qigong, or doing some sort of service work.

My rationale for this requirement is to enhance the presence of the teacher. I discussed this work, its rationale, and some outcomes of the practice in chapter 8. Besides the positive individual effects of doing practice, I believe that everyone doing practice contributes somehow to a deeper sense of community. This community is similar to what Chris-topher Bache (2008) calls a learning field. Over years of teaching at the postsecondary level, he has witnessed "learning fields" grow around the courses he teaches. He argues that a group energy develops that can affect subsequent classes. Bache teaches courses in religion at Youngstown State University in Ohio and has practised meditation himself for many years. He cites research to support his claim of learning fields, including the work of Dean Radin (2006). Bache (2008) suggests that a "learning field reflects and embodies the cumulative learning of all the students with a specific professor" (53). He makes the distinction between a learning field in a course, that is, course field, which develops over time, and the class field which is the current group he is teaching.

One of his students described her experience of the learning field:

All of us who have been in your classes felt a deep connection to one another. We don't know what it is. We only know that it is there. All that I know is that I have felt something binding us all together ... Imagine all of this taking place on a college campus. A college class that wasn't only a class it was community; semester after semester. (44)

This collective energy resides below conscious awareness but can impact learning in the classroom. One student described her experience of the learning field:

Instead of hearing your lectures with my Brain-Mind-Intellect, I actually heard you from somewhere else ... Heart-Soul maybe? Ears of a type that I hadn't been exercising. They had atrophied. You gave them a workout. Or the class field was so intense that it penetrated my controlling dominant brain-mind and vibrated my heart-soul like cardiac shock paddles to bring it to life.

The result? I'm becoming who I was *long* ago. The field by-passed my intellect and went directly to my heart to pry it open ... I now know what I had deeply buried in me for years, and the gift of folks in the classroom. It didn't come from me alone. (28)

The result of the learning field is what Bache (2008) calls *great learning*. Great learning is transformative and can reveal itself in many ways, including "when students write essays that surprise even themselves" (63). I have had similar experiences with my students, and a book I co-edited, *Teaching from the Thinking Heart: The Practice of Holistic Education* (Miller, Irwin, and Nigh 2014), includes twenty-two essays by students who took my course, the Holistic Curriculum. I believe that many of these essays are examples of "great learning."

This year one student wrote a paper entitled "Compassion Flows in Every Direction," which was about children of parents who experienced the Holocaust and how they cared for their parents. I cite a concluding paragraph:

I learned a great deal about compassion, care and love from my Israeli family's stories. I had not expected to focus on the transmission of love from child to adult. At school, the love from teacher to child seems to be the natural way of life; however, this mini-study has compelled me to look at how compassion flows in every direction. It has been my folly not to develop this awareness earlier. I have recognized how children, when they have their needs met, have a great capacity to care for adults both emotionally and physically. During the course of writing this paper, I have begun to look for the compassion, patience and forgiveness that students show their teachers in my school, and I have been so pleased to notice many instances. It is a great capacity that we are born with: when we feel loved, however imperfect that love may be, we respond with compassion and more love. It is a wonderful cycle.

This is a beautiful image of love flowing in every direction.

Another student wrote about his experience of love which came from coaching basketball. His high school team had finished second in a tournament. After the tournament he was riding on the bus with the team and he was overcome with an experience of love.

I was immersed in love. My students had taught me how to love the game. It was not our coach to player relationship that was working at that moment. It was the love for the game of basketball that brought us so far. I did not realize it until my mind was quiet. It was the same love that was all around me. It was everywhere and everything. My team played for all the kids who did not make it for the school and for others. My kids were singing, my heart was jumping out of my chest. Love was all around me it silenced me, humbled me and I could not believe I did not feel it sooner. It was loud, powerful and flowing through me. I began to tear up as I realized that I was transmitting that love for the game to all others I had interacted with that day. It was so revolutionary to think that I played a role in the development of basketball players who all had such a powerful love for the sport. I could feel the love of my many mentors who had helped me witness my success at the tournament. I could feel the wisdom of my elders who had experienced the love of coaching for such a long time and had helped me on my journey. They seemed like masters of this love who were showing me the door to it. Their love and our love were one and played a big role in this whole experience of love. Tears began to flow quicker and quicker I was happy no one could see me in the dark of the bus at night. I just broke down into tears of pure joy. It felt so natural to me, in fact as a child I used to cry all the time. It was revealed to me that I cried for the great joys and pains in my life. Love was behind the greatest joy and greatest pain. I thought of my grandfather who passed and I began to cry more. I had realized that I had seen him at his most joyful moment when he said good bye to his great-grand daughter. He didn't know it was the last time he would see her but it was. He was crying then too like I was crying now. The whole course of my life was embedded in this joy. I realized there was nothing wrong with my tears and as it was how I experienced love. I felt that my presence on that bus was not only a product of my love for basketball but the love that gave purpose to why I taught in the first place. The role of being ridiculed for my tears played in me becoming a teacher had me crying for joy now on this bus. I was at peace and all around me was love and I was so humbled to be a part of it. The love of the game was not just the love of basketball. It was the love of life. It was the love of our ancestors who had never even heard of basketball. Our love timelessly inextricable for the love of the game. I was not just coaching basketball. I was giving that love to game that was already loved by so many. Basketball was becoming a part of my story and the lessons of love I had learned from it was becoming a part of the lives of a countless number of people who continue to spread it. It was probably the most powerful yet unexpected feeling that I have experienced in my life. The miracle of revolution and transformation cannot be put into a single word. It must be felt.

I was honoured that the student would share this experience with me.

I refer again to Barbara Fredrickson's (2014) work, which I wrote about at the beginning of this book. More specifically she writes, "Love is the momentary upwelling of three tightly interwoven events: first, a sharing of one or more positive emotions between you and another; second, a synchrony between your and the other person's biochemistry and behaviors; and third, a reflected motive to invest in each other's well-being that brings mutual care" (17). This definition of love would help clarify what sometimes occurs in the classroom as Fredrickson argues that love occurs within interpersonal transactions that can arise in any group setting. She writes, "Love unfolds and reverberates between and among people" (19). This is what one student was experiencing when she wrote, "There is a lot of love in this room." Everyone in the class experiences this love differently and some not at all. Still it leads to what my student wrote which I cite again:

> Simply put, I feel this course is about healing one another. To me, it is "home" as it has been welcoming and inviting enough to allow me to develop close and intimate relationship with many people whom I had just met. I also find this course real, authentic and organic. It is first and foremost about us, one human being to another, about opening our hearts, reaching out and supporting one another, sharing our stories of joy and sorrow, our moments of vulnerability and allowing ourselves to feel empathy at a very deep and personal level.

Some of the student evaluations echoed this comment. One student wrote, "His (Jack's) loving energy creates the kind of space that allows students to explore safely. In this way, the students can bond. His emphasis on love is profound, absolutely necessary."

Vision for Education

Education that nurtures love can arise where there is connection, non-violence, curiosity, and presence. Reality at its core is interdependent and connected. The curriculum should be in harmony with that reality. Students need to experience this through a variety of connections. A connection can eventually lead to love whether it be love of knowledge or love of others. Experiences in nature can help young people see themselves as rooted in the processes of the earth. Gardens on or near school grounds can provide such experiences. I read a doctoral thesis where a teacher had a dog in her intermediate school classroom in Australia and how this animal made a difference in the lives of students (Nicholls 2011). The dog was named Gus after Saint Augustine, and Bernadette Nicholls (2011) writes how his presence nurtured love in the classroom:

> The Year 10 student from 2004 described their class being like *family*, which epitomizes love in the classroom. The selfless form of love that Gus shared seemed to invite the students to relate differently to each other, to become an "us" rather than class made up of small factional groups. Within this classroom *family*, students experienced a sense of connection through Gus and claimed he "helped them get to know each other more" and he "starts conversations." When Pete was asked what he missed about Gus after in class he said, "The love … the happiness." (220)

Nicholls also writes about how Gus helped create a better learning environment in the class. Of course, not all classes can have a dog, but we need different ways that nature can be a part of learning.

I have given the example of one school, Equinox, that bases its curriculum on connections. Of course, there are others and I believe Waldorf education and Montessori education can also foster love and well-being in students. Waldorf is also a model for how love of beauty can be central to learning and examples were presented in the chapter on beauty.

Learning about nonviolence and its history needs to become part of the curriculum. First, students need to see how the media, films, television, and so much of society glorify violence and thus contribute to suffering in the world. History textbooks are filled with descriptions of wars and sometimes glorify war. The curriculum needs to include people who resisted war and gave their lives to not participating in war, such as Gandhi, King, Aung San Suu Kyi, Thoreau, and others. In his book *To End All*

Wars, Adam Hochschild (2011) writes about an imaginary cemetery that would honour those "who understood war's madness enough not to take part" (376). Hochschild writes that these people knew in the short term their stance might be futile but tried to set an example for future generations. As one prisoner of conscience, Alice Wheldon, put it, "the world is my country." The study of nonviolence should not be presented as an ideology but as an area of inquiry.

Children's curiosity needs to be supported through a more relaxed curriculum that allows exploration. Let's face it, the need to "cover material" often can be a waste of time where students memorize material for a test then forget that material within a few days, never to be recalled. Let's explore ways that children's curiosity can be supported.

The presence of the teacher is fundamental to a classroom that is caring and compassionate. This presence can be developed through contemplative practices that should be included in pre-service and in-service teaching training programs. A caring and compassionate teacher naturally builds a classroom that is a loving community that students want to attend. Each student is honoured and respected for who he or she is. Contemplative practices and various body-mind practices such as qigong and yoga also can be introduced in the curriculum so that students can manage their own mental and physical well-being. These practices also support self-love, which forms the basis for loving others.

Finally, educators in North America need to look at the Nordic Theory of Love. We need to ask ourselves why children in those countries come out consistently higher on measures of health and well-being. What could be more important than the well-being of our children?

Appendix
Jack's Journey

In education, as in other areas, there is a lot of emphasis on the story. People are being encouraged to tell their stories as a way of interpreting or framing their own experiences. In my classes at the Ontario Institute for Studies in Education (OISE), I tell my own story. I do it in the spirit of Emerson (2003), when he wrote a story about a preacher, but we can substitute teacher, "He had lived in vain. He had no one word intimating that he had laughed or wept, was married or in love, had been commended, or cheated, or chagrined. If he had ever lived and acted, we were none the wiser for it" (257). I find that students welcome the opportunity to hear about my own journey, so I am closing the book with my own story.

I was born in 1943 and raised in Kansas City, Missouri, where my parents provided a loving and secure environment. My mother's name, Joy, was so appropriate, as she had a wonderful sense of humour. She could make me and others in her life laugh. I can remember many times in my childhood sharing a smile, a giggle, or a laugh. I was named after my father, John Miller, and because our names were the same my parents called me Jack. People who know me call me Jack while my writing is under John Miller and this sometimes causes confusion. My father, who seemed remote in my childhood, became a more important figure in my life during adolescence and young adulthood. We both liked sports, and we would talk a lot about baseball and particularly football at the University of Missouri where both my mother and father went to school. My father respected my right to make my own decisions, even though some of my choices were not those that he would have made. My grandmother was the other significant adult in my life. She introduced me to the wonder of music by giving me Beethoven's *Fifth Symphony* when I was in grade 6 and, to this day, I have found a spiritual connection in music, particularly the works of Mozart, Bach, and Haydn. My grandmother also introduced me to Tolstoy's spiritual writing when I was in high school. I had good friends growing up, but I also remember spending a lot of time by myself, as I particularly liked to read.

I have an older brother, Bill. Over the years we have grown closer. As I write this he has just taken on a faculty position at the University of Missouri's School of Medicine. Since we both attended the University of Missouri in Columbia, we follow the football and basketball teams every year.

I attended the University of Missouri for my BA and then went to Harvard in 1965 to pursue a Master of Arts in Teaching. It was in Boston that I met my first wife, Jean, whom I married in December 1967. Jean came from an Irish-Boston background that was so different from my Midwestern background, yet it was clear from the beginning that we were meant to be together.

Jean and I began our married life in the Midwest as I worked at Grinnell College in Iowa and later at the University of Missouri–Kansas City. Our first married year was that turbulent year of 1968. Like so many Americans I still remember vividly where we were when Martin Luther King Jr. and Bobby Kennedy were shot. I also recall that August when we were moving to Kansas City where I would begin a job teaching at the University of Missouri–Kansas City (UMKC). The Russians had invaded Czechoslovakia, and when we were settling into our new apartment in Kansas City, we watched the riots at the Democratic convention in Chicago on television. The debates between Gore Vidal and William Buckley, I felt, characterized the deep divisions of that time.

That year of 1968 I began my spiritual search. I had been raised a Christian (Disciples of Christ), but as I confronted the draft and the Vietnam War, I needed something more in order to deal with the anxiety I was feeling. I had filed a Conscientious Objector statement that was not declaring myself as a pacifist but directing my criticism against U.S. intervention in Vietnam. I quoted Henry David Thoreau (1983) in my statement:

> It is not a man's duty as a matter of course, to devote himself to the eradication of any, even the most enormous wrong; he may still properly have other concerns to engage him; but it is his duty, at least to wash his hands of it ... If the injustice is part of the necessary friction of the machine of government, let it go ... but if it is of such nature that it requires you to be the agent of injustice to another, then I say, break the law. (396)

Thoreau and Emerson have been two of my teachers throughout my life (Miller 2011). Since I believed that the U.S. intervention was wrong, I was prepared to resist the draft and thus break the law. Jean and I had decided that if I was inducted, we would go to Canada. The possibility of such a change in my life created a tremendous amount of stress. I suffered from dizzy spells and nervous tension. The stress began to interfere with my work at UMKC so I began to look for ways to deal with my problems. Sometime during that fall, I read Jess Stearn's *Yoga, Youth and Reincarnation* (1965), which described some simple hatha yoga exercises that I began to practise every day. Within weeks I began to feel more relaxed. In short, the draft started me on my spiritual journey. I became interested in the spiritual framework that underpinned yoga, and I began reading about Eastern spiritual practices.

I received my induction notice in April of 1969, and Jean and I began to make our plans to go to Canada. We emigrated to Toronto in June of that year, and I began my doctoral studies in education at the Ontario Institute of Studies in Education at the University of Toronto. The pain of leaving my parents that June morning is still vivid in my memory, as I can still see them standing sadly at the door as Jean and I drove away. When we arrived in Toronto the next day, we found that our furniture hadn't reached our apartment, so Jean and I bought air mattresses and army blankets so we could sleep in our unusually cold apartment. That summer I alternated between exhilaration and depression, as I felt "at home" in Canada, yet I often became depressed at the thought that I might never again be able to travel to the U.S. to see my family. In a sense, going to Canada was like a death, because I had to let go of so much.

Eventually, we settled into life in Toronto. Our first child, Patrick, was born there in 1970. When I graduated, I took a job in Thunder Bay, Ontario, working with the Ontario Institute for Studies in Education in their field office. My work involved working with schools in a consultant's capacity. Thunder Bay is located 200 miles north of Duluth, Minnesota, and is relatively isolated. Snow settles on the ground in November and doesn't leave until the beginning of April.

Helping me through these difficult years of change was my wife, Jean. Her warmth and love provided the support that carried me through these transitions. We both began to see our marriage as a spiritual partnership or a mutual environment for our spiritual growth. Jean also did yoga and we both shared an interest in Eastern spirituality. The teachings of Ram Dass were helpful to us, and I can still remember us falling to sleep at night listening to his words on tape. We both began to see that our lives had a meaning and purpose and that we were connected to something much larger than ourselves. It was through the Ram Dass literature that I learned of the work of Joseph Goldstein and Jack Kornfield, who introduced

Buddhist meditation to many people in North America. In 1974 I ordered a set of tapes by Joseph Goldstein on meditation instruction. These tapes provided the beginning of my own meditation practice, which I have continued to this day.

In 1976 Jean's father died, and in 1977 my mother passed away. The works of Elizabeth Kübler-Ross were very helpful to Jean and me, and gave us a framework for understanding and working with the pain of these losses. She helped us see death as another transition rather than as the end. At the same time, joy came with the birth of our daughter, Nancy, in 1976.

Another watershed year for Jean and me was 1982. I attended my first meditation retreat at Barre, Massachusetts, which was conducted by Jack Kornfield and Sharon Salzburg. The retreat was two weeks long and consisted of alternating sitting meditation with walking meditation throughout the day. Much of the retreat was spent sitting in pain as my knees and legs ached. However, halfway through the retreat, I felt a sense of joy and rapture that permeated my whole being. These two weeks helped me deepen my practice.

Shortly after Christmas that year Jean told me she had a lump in her breast. I couldn't believe that she might have cancer. I remember that time as one where she went for tests and I read as much as possible about the disease. We got a call one Sunday morning in January to say she should come in that day for her surgery that would take place the next day. Oh, how low I felt as I drove her to the hospital. After the operation she lay in the room and I sat with her as I waited for her to awaken. As I looked at her, I felt such compassion and realized that we were connected beyond time and space. Up until this point we had a wonderful marriage based on love and trust, but now we started on a journey that resulted in spiritual union.

She recovered rapidly from the surgery and her usual buoyant spirits returned. I remember her swinging her arm around two days after the surgery to show me how good she felt. The prognosis, however, wasn't good since the cancer had spread to the lymph nodes. She had to have chemotherapy and the treatments became increasingly more difficult as she lost her hair and she was nauseous after each treatment. However, at the end of the treatments, she bounced back. The work of Bernie Siegel was very helpful to Jean as she began her fight with cancer.

At this time we moved to St. Catharines in southern Ontario, where Jean loved her new home and surroundings. She reached out to make new friends, and she completed her undergraduate honours degree in psychology at Brock University. There was no evidence of any recurrence of the cancer for almost three years.

In September of 1986, however, we began our final journey together. I knew something was wrong when she had trouble remembering simple words. One morning I was going out shopping and she couldn't remember the word "muffin" and I cried out to her, "What's happening?" In a couple of weeks, her memory got worse and we rushed to the doctor's. He ordered an emergency CAT scan. We learned in a few days that the cancer had spread to the brain and that Jean had to undergo radiation treatment for two weeks. For several weeks Jean could hardly express herself, and I had to be with her constantly. However, worse was to come as she became very weak from the treatments, and she lay sleeping on the couch except to get up for meals. She slept almost around the clock for six weeks; her legs became very thin. Around Christmas she began to recover, as she gained energy and her memory improved. In January, it looked like she might fully recover when we received more devastating news – the cancer had spread to her lung. She now began a new round of chemotherapy treatments. She handled these treatments very well and began to return to a normal lifestyle. The cancer was in remission. We were able to travel to Florida in March of 1987, and she was horseback riding in late April. People marvelled at her spirits and how she recovered. Jean had hardly been able to walk in December, and in April she was living a normal life and horseback riding, even while she was still taking the chemotherapy treatments.

The real miracle, however, was that there was a spiritual awakening that paralleled her awakening from her long rest in November and December. The last year of her life Jean lived in Christ Consciousness. Despite the pain and fear, her eyes radiated a warmth and glow that came from her spiritual heart. She was totally centred in a way that she had never been until she became sick. I remember her saying so often, even in the midst of her cancer, "I feel so blessed." Throughout our marriage Jean said that I was her teacher, but in the last year of her life, she became my teacher. I marvelled at her courage and spiritual presence. The cancer made me surrender completely to what was happening. Meditation practice proved invaluable, as in our practice we have to witness pain in our bodies. By accepting pain in ourselves, we learn to be present to pain in others.

We got more bad news that fall when we learned that the cancer had spread to the liver. She was treated again with chemotherapy. Again she seemed to sail through the treatments, and we spent a wonderful

Christmas together that year. We went to Florida with the kids in March and, as Jean walked the beach, she remarked "this is heaven." She always loved the ocean and was most joyful and peaceful when she was near the water. I couldn't have dreamed then that she would die in a few weeks. Jean's approach to life at that time was like the Zen story of the man who was hanging from a cliff facing certain death below when his grip finally tired. Despite the presence of death, the man reached out to take a strawberry growing on the cliff side and savoured each mouthful as he ate it. Jean, who knew that she was going to die, savoured each moment with her family, whom she loved so deeply.

Jean died at home on April 11, 1988, where she wanted to be. She needed only Tylenol for the pain those last days. Despite the cancer, she always felt blessed because of her family and the love that they returned to her. A few minutes after Jean died, my son, Patrick, came into the room and hugged his mother. I sat with Jean that evening and waited for the doctor to come to pronounce her dead. I read passages from Stephen Levine's (1989) book that help a soul move into the light. When the undertaker came, Nancy and Patrick picked out an outfit for their mother. I was amazed at the strength and calmness they showed in the presence of death.

It was through Jean that I learned about the fundamentals of life – suffering, love, and death. It was through this experience that the teachings of Buddha and Christ came alive. However, in the end it was clear that my wife, Jean, had become my most powerful and wisest teacher. Our marriage could be viewed as a spiritual partnership where we helped each other through our respective crises so that we could touch the oneness.

Since Jean's death, I have been married twice. Both these women have also been my teachers. Susan Drake, a professor at Brock University, taught me about the importance of taking care of my body. Up until I met Susan I never exercised, but my walks with her showed how I needed to respect the body. We also worked together on various books and articles in holistic education. Finally, she helped me navigate the difficult years after Jean's death. Recently, my daughter, Nancy, learned that she had breast cancer. Susan was very much saddened by this news and has continued to share her concern and support for my daughter during this difficult time.

Both my children are very dear to me. My son, Patrick, is a professor in philosophy at Duquesne University in Pittsburgh, Pennsylvania, and his wife, Sarah, has given birth to my two grandchildren, Simon and Mary Jean. Patrick is a model parent and I admire how he cares for his children. My son and I share an interest in politics and sports.

My daughter, Nancy, has just completed a PhD in Creative Writing and Dance at Roehampton University in London. Nancy carries a gene mutation inherited from her mother and contracted breast cancer in 2012 while she was in London. She bravely dealt with her disease by turning to her artistic and spiritual practices, namely yoga, writing, and dance to help her get through. Nancy has studied and taught yoga and meditation since 2005. Nancy is a published poet and teaches courses on contemplative and creative arts (nancy@nancyellenmiller.com).

I am now married to Midori Sakurai whom I met in Japan when I was giving talks there in 1994. Midori is a healing presence in my life and has been a real help to my children and grandchildren. She has travelled to Pittsburgh to help my son's family shortly after each of their children were born. I usually go to Japan every year to teach a course in holistic education at Kobe Shinwa Women's University and Midori translates for me. We enjoy working together there. Midori also makes beautiful objects out of wool through felting (http://midostail-felt.blogspot.ca). She has been my teacher as well and one of the many things she has taught me is to appreciate animals.

When this book is published, I will be seventy-four. I am still teaching and continue to draw inspiration from the students I work with. I am very grateful that I have been able to introduce contemplative practices to my students and to have supervised several doctoral theses on contemplative education. Teaching and working with young people continue to bring much joy into my life. I see no reason to retire as long as this is true.

Readings and Online Resources

Readings

Ackerman, Peter, and Duvall, Jack. 2000. *A Force More Powerful: A Century of Nonviolent Conflict*. New York: Palgrave. A comprehensive history of nonviolence.

Armstrong, Karen. 2011. *Twelve Steps to a Compassionate Life*. New York: Knopf. Armstrong is one of leading advocates for living compassionately. This book is a helpful guide.

Berry, Thomas. 1988. *The Dream of the Earth*. San Francisco: Sierra Club Books. A beautiful and moving description of our planet and how human beings can consciously inhabit and care for the earth.

Birx, Ellen. 2014. *Selfless Love: Beyond the Boundaries of Self and Other*. Boston: Wisdom. Writing from a Buddhist perspective, Birx describes how meditation can be a path to love.

Carroll, Linda. 2014. *Love Cycles: The Five Essential Stages of Lasting Love*. Novato, CA: New World Library. Carroll describes stages of long-term relationships that can reach the last stage of wholehearted love.

Engel, Susan. 2015. *The Hungry Mind: The Origins of Curiosity in Childhood*. Cambridge, MA: Harvard University Press. This is an up-to-date and valuable contribution to literature on curiosity. Includes suggestions for teachers and schools.

Fredrickson, Barbara L. 2014. *Love 2.0: Creating Happiness and Health in Moments of Connection*. New York: Plume. This book describes how love can arise in groups and she also provides several exercises for helping create positive conditions for love to arise.

Frenkel, Edward. 2013. *Love and Math: The Heart of Hidden Reality*. New York: Basic Books. Frenkel makes a powerful case for mathematics and how it is a path to the hidden reality underlying the universe.

Gordon, Mary. 2005. *Roots of Empathy: Changing the World Child by Child.* Toronto: Thomas Allen. This book describes a program that has been used in schools that develops empathy in children.

Hardin, Moh. 2015. *A Little Book of Love.* Boston: Shambhala. Hardin describes how meditation can be a path to self-love.

hooks, bell. 2000. *All about Love: New Visions.* New York: Harper. hooks develops an "ethic" of love that can guide our lives. Essential reading.

Hunt, David. 2010. *To Be a Friend: The Key to Friendship in Our Lives.* Toronto: Dundurn. A practical guide about how to be friend to yourself and others. Contains many activities that support being a friend.

King, Martin Luther Jr. 1981. *Strength to Love.* Philadelphia: Fortress Press. This is King's major work on nonviolence and his belief in the power of love.

Lewis, C.S. 1960. *The Four Loves.* New York: Harcourt Brace. Writing from a Christian perspective, Lewis describes four types of love: affection, friendship, Eros, and charity.

Makransky, John. 2007. *Awakening through Love: Unveiling Your Deepest Goodness.* Boston: Wisdom. Working from the perspective of Tibetan Buddhism, Makransky is an inspiring guide to how we can bring love into our lives.

Merton, Thomas. 1965. *Love and Living.* New York: Harcourt Brace. Merton, the Catholic contemplative, writes about how "love is our true destiny."

Miller, John P. 2007. *The Holistic Curriculum.* Toronto: University of Toronto Press. Describes how curriculum can be built on connections. Provides the framework for the Equinox Holistic Alternative School.

Nagler, Michael. 2004. *The Search for a Nonviolent Future: A Promise of Peace for Ourselves, Our Families and Our World.* Novato, CA: New World Library. Essential reading on nonviolence. Filled with ideas of how we can bring nonviolence into our lives and our communities.

Noddings, Nel. 1992. *The Challenge to Care in Schools: An Alternative Approach to Education.* New York: Teachers College Press. Noddings has written extensively on caring and this book provides practical ways of bringing care into classrooms.

O'Donohue, John. 2004. *The Invisible Embrace: Beauty.* New York: Harper Perennial. O'Donohue describes beauty from a variety of perspectives and discusses how it can be a part of daily life.

Ricard, Matthieu. 2015. *Altruism: The Power of Compassion to Change Yourself and the World.* New York: Little, Brown, and Co. A comprehensive text on compassion, empathy and lovingkindness.

Smalley, Susan L., and Diana Winston. 2010. *Fully Present: The Science, Art and Practice of Mindfulness.* Boston: DeCapo. One of best books on mindfulness, presenting research as well as exercises.

Online Resources

Karen Armstrong and the Charters

Information about Karen Armstrong's work can be found at https://www. charterforcompassion.org.

Karen Armstrong's Charter for Compassion can be found at https:// www.charterforcompassion.org/images/menus/charter/pdfs/ CharterFlyer10-30-2012_0.pdf.

Charter for Compassionate Schools can be found at https://www. charterforcompassion.org/index.php/charter-for-compassionate-schools.

Children's Charter for Compassion can be found at http://www. childrenscharterforcompassion.com.

Additional Online Resources

Heart-Mind Online (http://heartmindonline.org) is a website developed by the Dalai Lama Center for Peace and Education. It is for anyone searching for evidenced-informed resources that educate the hearts of children. The collection of resources builds capacity in individuals and communities to support the development of the hearts and minds of children, and promotes their positive social and emotional development.

CASEL (Collaborative for Academic, Social and Emotional Learning; http:// www.casel.org) the largest social and emotional learning (SEL) think tank in the world. CASEL's mission is to help make SEL an integral part of education from preschool through high school. All you want to know about SEL programs.

Greater Good Science Center (http://greatergood.berkeley.edu) studies the psychology, sociology, and neuroscience of well-being, and teaches skills that foster a thriving, resilient, and compassionate society. Many excellent articles on mindfulness in education.

Edutopia (https://www.edutopia.org) is a large U.S. non-profit that shares evidence- and practitioner-based learning strategies that empower you to improve K–12 education. Many articles on mindfulness, and on social and emotional learning.

References

Ackerman, Peter, and Jack Duvall. 2000. *A Force More Powerful: A Century of Nonviolent Conflict*. New York: Palgrave.

Alcott, Amos Bronson. 1872. *Concord Days*. Boston: Roberts Brothers.

Alexander, Eben. 2012. *Proof of Heaven: A Neurosurgeon's Journey into the Afterlife*. New York: Simon and Schuster.

Alighieri, Dante. 2003. *The Divine Comedy*. Translated by John Ciardi. New York: New American Library.

Armstrong, Karen. 2010. *Twelve Steps to a Compassionate Life*. New York: Knopf.

Bache, Christopher M. 2008. *The Living Classroom: Teaching and Collective Consciousness*. Albany, NY: SUNY Press.

Baldwin, Carol. 1994. *Calling the Circle: The First and Future Culture*. Newberg, OR: Swan, Raven and Co.

Barron, Frank, and David M. Harrington. 1981. "Creativity, Intelligence, and Personality." *Annual Review of Psychology* 32 (1): 439–76. https://doi.org/10.1146/annurev.ps.32.020181.002255.

Batson, C. Daniel. 2009. "These Things Called Empathy: Eight Related but Distinct Phenomena." In *The Social Neuroscience of Empathy*, edited by Jean Decety and William Ickes, 3–15. Cambridge, MA: MIT Press. https://doi.org/10.7551/mitpress/9780262012973.003.0002.

Berry, Thomas. 1988. *The Dream of the Earth*. San Francisco: Sierra Club Books.

Birx, Ellen. 2014. *Selfless Love: Beyond the Boundaries of Self and Other*. Boston: Wisdom.

Bloom, Allan. 1993. *Love & Friendship*. New York: Simon and Schuster.

Boulding, Kenneth E. 1989. *Three Faces of Power*. Newbury Park, CA: Sage.

Boyce, Barry, ed. 2011. "Creating a Mindful Society." In *The Mindfulness Revolution*, edited by Barry Boyce, 252–64. Boston: Shambhala.

Brahm, Ajahn. 2011. *The Art of Disappearing: The Buddha's Path to Lasting Joy.* Summerville, MA: Wisdom.

Brown, Keith. 2017. "Loving Kindness Meditation: Awakening Teacher Eros in Modern Educational Settings." In *Holistic Education and Embodied Learning*, edited by John Miller and Kelli Nigh, 175–200. Charlotte, NC: Information Age Publishing.

Bucke, Richard Maurice. 1982. *Cosmic Consciousness: A Study in the Evolution of the Human Mind.* Secaucus, NJ: Citadel Press.

Capra, Fritjof. 1996. *The Web of Life: A New Scientific Understanding of Living Systems.* New York: Doubleday.

Carroll, Linda. 2014. *Love Cycles: The Five Essential Stages of Lasting Love.* Novato, CA: New World Library.

Chadwick, David. 1999. *Crooked Cucumber: The Life and Zen Teachings of Shunryu Suzuki.* New York: Broadway Books.

Cohen, Avraham. 2015. *Becoming Fully Human within Educational Environments: Inner Life, Relationship, and Learning.* Burnaby, BC: White Room Press.

Cohen, Warren, and Brian Bresnihan. 2017. "The Art of Education: Waldorf Education in Practice." In *Holistic Education and Embodied Learning*, edited by John P. Miller and Kelli Nigh, 77–102. Charlotte, NC: Information Age Publishing.

Csikszentmihalyi, Mihaly. 1997. *Finding Flow: The Psychology of Engagement with Everyday Life.* New York: Basic Books.

Davidson, Richard J., with Sharon Begley. 2012. *The Emotional Life of Your Brain.* New York: Hudson Street Press.

Dellinger, David. 1993. *From Yale to Jail: The Life of a Moral Dissenter.* New York: Pantheon.

DeLoache, Judy S., Gabrielle Simcock, and Suzanne Macari. 2007. "Planes, Trains, Automobiles and Tea Sets: Extremely Intense Interests in Very Young Children." *Developmental Psychology* 43 (6): 1579–86. https://doi.org/10.1037/0012-1649.43.6.1579.

de Nicolás, Antonio T. 1989. *Habits of Mind: An Introduction to Philosophy.* New York: Paragon.

Easwaran, Eknath. 1999. *Nonviolent Soldier of Islam: Badshah Khan: A Man to Match His Mountains.* 2nd ed. Petaluma, CA: Nilgiri Press.

Emerson, Ralph Waldo. [1940] 1968. *The Selected Writings of Ralph Waldo Emerson.* Edited by Brooks Atkinson. New York: The Modern Library.

Emerson, Ralph Waldo. 1982. *Emerson in His Journals*. Edited by Joel Porte. Cambridge, MA: Belknap Press.

Emerson, Ralph Waldo. 2003. *Selected Writings*. New York: Signet Classic.

Engel, Susan. 2015. *The Hungry Mind: The Origins of Curiosity in Childhood*. Cambridge, MA: Harvard University Press. https://doi.org/10.4159/9780674425354.

Erikson, Erik. 1993. *Childhood and Society*. New York: W.W. Norton.

Farrell, John H. 2012. *Clarence Darrow*. New York: Random House.

Ferrini, Paul. 2016. *Daily Wisdom from Paul Ferrini*. 27 June. https://www.paulferrini.com.

Fidyk, A. 2009. "A 'Rehabilitation of Eros': Cultivating a Conscious Relation with Love." *Jung Journal: Culture & Psyche* 3 (4): 59–68. https://doi.org/10.1525/jung.2009.3.4.59.

Finser, Torin M. 1994. *Schools as a Journey: The Eight-Year Odyssey of a Waldorf Teacher and His Class*. Hudson, NY: Anthroposohic Press.

Fischer, Louis. 1954. *Gandhi: His Life and Message for the World*. New York: Mentor.

Fox, Nathan A., Heather A. Henderson, Koraly Perez-Edgar, and Lasren K. White. 2008. "The Biology of Temperament: An Integrative Approach." In *Handbook of Developmental Cognitive Neuroscience*, 92nd ed., edited by Charles. A Nelson and Monica Luciana, 839–53. Cambridge, MA: MIT Press.

Frady, Marshall. 1992. "1992 "The Outsider, II: History is Upon Us." *The New Yorker* (10 February): 41.

Fredrickson, Barbara L. 2014. *Love 2.0: Creating Happiness and Health in Moments of Connection*. New York: Plume.

Frenkel, Edward. 2013. *Love and Math: The Heart of Hidden Reality*. New York: Basic Books.

Fulton, Crystal. 2009. "The Pleasure Principle: The Power of Positive Affect in Information Seeking." *Aslib Proceedings* 61 (3): 245–61. https://doi.org/10.1108/00012530910959808.

Gandhi, Mahatma. 1980. *All Men Are Brothers: Autobiographical Reflections*. Edited by Krishna Kripalani. New York: Continuum.

Gandhi, Mahatma. 1999. *The Collected Works of Mahatma Gandhi (Electronic Book)*. 98 vols. New Delhi: Publications Division Government of India.

Gandhi, Mahatma. 2011. *Gandhi: An Autobiography*. Toronto: Fitzhenry and Whiteside.

Garrow, David J. 1986. *Bearing the Cross: Martin Luther King, Jr. and the Southern Christian Leadership Conference*. New York: Morrow.

Gildiner, Catherine. 2015. *Coming Ashore*. Toronto: ECW Press.

Goethe, Johann von. [1810] 1970. *Theory of Colours*. Cambridge, MA: MIT Press.

Gordon, Mary. 2005. *Roots of Empathy: Changing the World Child by Child*. Toronto: Thomas Allen.

Gougeon, Len. 2007. *Emerson and Eros: The Making of a Cultural Hero*. Albany, NY: State University of New York Press.

Gray, Peter. 2013. *Free to Learn: Why Unleashing the Instinct to Play Will Make Our Children Happier, More Self-Reliant, and Better Students for Life*. New York: Basic Books.

Griffin, Robert. 1977. "Discipline: What's It Taking Out of You?" *Learning* (February): 77–80.

Hadot, Pierre. 2002. *What Is Ancient Philosophy?* Cambridge, MA: Harvard University Press.

Hall, Debbie. 2007. "The Power of Presence." In *This I Believe: The Personal Philosophies of Remarkable Men and Women*, edited by Jay Allison and Dan Gediman, 100–2. New York: Henry Holt.

Hanh, Thich Nhat. 1976. *The Miracle of Mindfulness! A Manual on Meditation*. Boston: Beacon Press.

Hanh, Thich Nhat. 1993. *Interbeing: Fourteen Guidelines for Engaged Buddhism*. Berkeley, CA: Parallax Press.

Hanh, Thich Nhat. 2016. *At Home in the World: Stories and Essential Teachings from a Monk's Life*. Berkeley, CA: Parallax Press.

Hardin, Moh. 2011. *A Little Book of Love*. Boston: Shambhala.

Hillman, Anne. 2008. *Awakening the Energies of Love: Discovering Fire for the Second Time*. Wilton Manors, FL: Bramble Books.

Hochschild, Adam. 2011. *To End All Wars: A Story of Loyalty and Rebellion, 1914–1918*. Boston: Mariner Books.

hooks, bell. 2000. *All about Love: New Visions*. New York: Harper.

Howe, Randy, ed. 2003. *The Quotable Teacher*. Guilford, CT: Lyons Press.

Hunt, David. 2010. *To Be a Friend: The Key to Friendship in Our Lives*. Toronto: Dundurn.

Hutcherson, Cendri A., Emma M. Seppala, and James J. Gross. 2008. "Loving-Kindness Meditation Increases Social Connectedness." *Emotion* 8 (5): 720–4.

Irwin, Michele, and John P. Miller. 2016. "Presence of Mind: A Qualitative Study of Meditating Teachers." *Journal of Transformative Education* 14 (2): 86–97. https://doi.org/10.1177/1541344615611257.

Isaacson, Walter. 2007. *Einstein: His Life and Universe*. New York: Simon and Schuster.

Jackson, Phil. 1995. *Sacred Hoops: Spiritual Lessons of a Hardwood Warrior*. New York: Hyperion.

Johnson, Robert. 1991. *Owning Your Own Shadow: Understanding the Dark Side of the Psyche*. San Francisco: Harper.

Kabat-Zinn, Jon. 1990. *Full Catastrophe Living: Using the Wisdom of Your Body and Mind to Face Stress, Pain and Illness*. New York: Delacorte Press.

Kang, Min J., Ming Hsu, Ian M. Krajbich, George Loewenstein, Samuel M. McClure, Joseph Tao-yi Wang, and Colin F. Camerer. 2009. "The Wick in the Candle of Learning: Epistemic Curiosity Activates Reward Circuitry and Enhances Memory." *Psychological Science* 20 (8): 963–73. https://doi.org/10.1111/j.1467-9280.2009.02402.x.

Keats, John. 1958. *The Selected Letters of John Keats*. Edited by Grant F. Scott. Cambridge, MA: Harvard University Press.

Kelley, Kevin W. 1988. *The Home Planet*. New York: Addison Wesley.

Kessler, Rachael. 2000. "The Teaching Presence." *Virginia Journal of Education* 94 (2): 7–10.

Kessler, Rachael. 2002. "Eros and the Erotic Shadow in Teaching and Learning." In *Nurturing Our Wholeness*, edited by John P. Miller and Yoshiharu Nakagawa, 267–84. Brandon, VT: Foundation for Educational Renewal.

Kessler, Rachael. 2009. The Teaching Presence. Unpublished paper. In possession of the author.

Knobloch, Silvia, Grit Patzig, Anna-Maria Mende, and Mathias Hastall. 2004. "Affective News: Effects of Discourse Structure in Narratives on Suspense, Curiosity and Enjoyment while Reading News and Novels." *Communication Research* 31 (3): 259–87. https://doi.org/10.1177/0093650203261517.

Kurlansky, Mark. 2008. *Nonviolence: The History of a Dangerous Idea*. New York: The Modern Library.

Lawrence, D.H. 1993. *Lady Chatterley's Lover and A Propos of 'Lady Chatterley's Lover*. Edited by Michael Squires. Cambridge: Cambridge University Press.

Leong, Kenneth. 2001. *The Zen Teachings of Jesus*. New York: Crossroad.

Leslie, Ian. 2014. *Curious: The Desire to Know and Why Your Future Depends on It*. Toronto: Anansi.

Levine, Stephen. 1989. *Who Dies: An Investigation of Conscious Living and Conscious Dying*. New York: Anchor.

Lillard, Angeline S. 2008. *Montessori: The Science behind the Genius*. New York: Oxford University Press.

Lin, Jing. 2006. *Love, Peace and Wisdom in Education: A Vision for Education in the Twenty-First Century*. Toronto: Rowman and Littlefield Education.

Liston, Daniel. 2000. "Love and Despair in Teaching." *Educational Theory* 50 (1): 81–102. https://doi.org/10.1111/j.1741-5446.2000.00081.x.

Long, Jeffrey. 2010. *Evidence of the Afterlife: The Science of Near-Death Experiences*. New York: Harper.

Lusseryan, Jacques. 1987. *And There Was Light*. New York: Parabola.

Lynd, Staughton, and Alice Lynd. 1995. *Nonviolence in America: A Documentary History*. Maryknoll, NY: Orbis.

Makransky, John. 2007. *Awakening through Love: Unveiling Your Deepest Goodness*. Boston: Wisdom.

Mani, Tatanga. 1972. *Touch the Earth: A Self-Portrait of Indian Existence*. Edited by T.C. McLuhan. New York: Pocket Books. 106.

McGilchrist, Iain. 2009. *The Master and the Emissary: The Divided Brain and the Making of the Western World*. New Haven, CT: Yale University Press.

McLuhan, T.C. 1972. *Touch the Earth: A Self-Portrait of Indian Existence*. New York: Pocket Books.

Miller, John P. 1988. *Spiritual Pilgrims*. Unpublished manuscript. In possession of the author.

Miller, John P. 2006. *Educating for Wisdom and Compassion: Creating Conditions for Timeless Learning*. Thousand Oaks, CA: Corwin.

Miller, John P. 2007. *The Holistic Curriculum*. Toronto: University of Toronto Press.

Miller, John P. 2010. *Whole Child Education*. Toronto: University of Toronto Press.

Miller, John P. 2011. *Transcendental Learning: The Educational Legacy of Alcott, Emerson, Fuller, Peabody and Thoreau*. Charlotte, NC: Information Age Publishing.

Miller, John P. 2016. "Equinox: Portrait of a Holistic School." *International Journal of Children's Spirituality* 21 (3–4): 283–301. https://doi.org/10.1080/1 364436X.2016.1232243.

Miller, John P., and Aya Nozawa. 2002. "Meditating Teachers: A Qualitative Study." *Journal of In-service Education* 28 (1): 179–92. https://doi.org/10.1080/13674580200200201.

Miller, John P., and Aya Nozawa. 2005. "Contemplation and Teaching." *Encounter: Education for Meaning and Social Justice* 18 (1): 42–8.

Miller, John P., Michele Irwin, and Kelli Nigh, eds. 2014. *Teaching from the Thinking Heart: The Practice of Holistic Education*. Charlotte, NC: Information Age Publishing.

Ming-Dao, Deng. 1992. *365 Tao: Daily Meditations*. San Francisco: HarperCollins.

Mitchell, Stephen. 1991. *The Gospel According to Jesus*. New York: HarperCollins.

Monks of New Skete. 1999. *In the Spirit of Happiness*. Boston: Little and Brown.

Moore, Thomas. 1992. *Care of the Soul: A Guide for Cultivating Depth and Sacredness in Everyday Life*. New York: Walker & Co. Large Print Edition.

Moore, Thomas. 2016. *Gospel: The Book of Matthew*. Woodstock, VT: Skylight.

Moorjani, Anita. 2012. *Dying to Be Me: My Journey from Cancer to Near Death to True Healing*. New York: Hay House.

Nagler, Michael. 2004. *The Search for a Nonviolent Future: A Promise of Peace for Ourselves, Our Families and Our World*. Novato, CA: New World Library.

Needleman, Jacob. 1996. *A Little Book on Love*. New York: Doubleday.

Neill, Alexander Sutherland. 1997. *Summerhill: A Radical Approach to Childrearing*. New York: Pocket Books.

Nicholls, Bernadette. 2011. "What's a Dog Got to Do with Education? Illuminating What Matters in Education and in Life." PhD diss., Latrobe University, Bundoora, Victoria.

Nielsen, Kim E. 2009. *Beyond the Miracle Worker*. Boston: Beacon Press.

Nikam, N., and R. McKeon. 1959. *Edicts of Ashoka*. Chicago: University of Chicago Press.

O'Donohue, John. 2004. *The Invisible Embrace: Beauty*. New York: Harper Perennial.

Partanen, Anu. 2016. *The Nordic Theory of Everything: In Search of a Better Life*. New York: HarperCollins.

Paz, Octavia. 1993. *The Double Flame: Love and Eroticism*. New York: Harcourt.

Phillips, Christopher. 2007. *Socrates in Love: Philosophy for a Passionate Heart*. New York: Norton.

Pidgeon, Sean. 2013. "Rapturous Research." Opinion Pages. *The New York Times*, 5 January. https://opinionator.blogs.nytimes.com/2013/01/05/rapturous-research/.

Plato. 2006. *Symposium* and *Phaedrus*. In *Plato on Love*, edited by C.D.C. Reeve. Indianapolis, IN: Hackett Publishing.

Popham, Peter. 2012. *The Lady and the Peacock: The Life of Aung San Suu Kyi*. New York: Experiment.

Radin, Dean. 2006. *Entangled Minds*. New York: Pocket Books.

Ricard, Matthieu. 2015. *Altruism: The Power of Compassion to Change Yourself and the World*. New York: Little, Brown, and Co.

Rich, Bruce. 2010. *To Uphold the World: A Call for a New Global Ethic from Ancient India*. Boston: Beacon.

Richards, Mary Caroline. 1980. *Toward Wholeness: Rudolf Steiner Education in America*. Middleton, CT: Wesleyan University.

Ross-Zainotz, Rebecca. 2012. "Mindfulness: A Reflection on Spiritual Practice." Unpublished student paper. In possession of the author.

Sagarin, Stephen. 1992. "Art in a Waldorf School." *Holistic Education Review* 5: 19–24.

Sahlberg, Pasi. 2011. *Finnish Lessons: What Can the World Learn from Educational Change in Finland*. New York: Teachers College Press.

Salzberg, Sharon. 1995. *Lovingkindness: The Revolutionary Art of Happiness*. Boston: Shambhala.

Schon, Donald A. 1983. *The Reflective Practitioner: How Professionals Think in Action*. New York: Basic Books.

Schorr, Daniel. 1993. "TV Violence: What We Know but Ignore." *The Christian Science Monitor* (7 September): 19. http://www.csmonitor.com/1993/0907/07191.html.

Schucman, Helen. 1975. *A Course in Miracles*. Huntington Station, NY: Foundation for Inner Peace.

Sharp, Gene. 2012. *From Dictatorship to Democracy: A Conceptual Framework for Liberation*. London: Serpent's Tail.

Siegel, Daniel. 2011. "The Proven Benefits of Mindfulness." In *The Mindfulness Revolution*, edited by Barry Boyce, 136–9. Boston: Shambhala.

Silvia, Paul. 2006. *Exploring the Psychology of Interest*. New York: Oxford University Press. https://doi.org/10.1093/acprof:oso/9780195158557.001.0001.

Smalley, Susan L., and Diana Winston. 2010. *Fully Present: The Science, Art and Practice of Mindfulness*. Boston: DeCapo.

Stearn, Jess. 1965. *Yoga, Youth and Reincarnation*. New York: Doubleday.

Steel, Sean. 2014. *The Pursuit of Wisdom and Happiness in Education: Historical Sources and Contemplative Practices*. Albany, NY: SUNY Press.

Stigler, James W., and Harold Stevenson. 1991. "How Asian Teachers Polish Each Lesson to Perfection." *American Educator* 15 (1): 12–20.

Suu Kyi, Aung San. 1997. *The Voice of Hope: Conversations with Alan Clements*. New York: Seven Stories Press.

Taylor, Jill Bolte. 2009. *My Stroke of Insight: A Brain Scientist's Personal Journey*. New York: Plume.

Tennov, Dorothy. 1979. *Love and Limerence: The Experience of Being in Love*. New York: Stein and Day.

Thomsen, Robert. 1975. *Bill W.* Center City, MN: Hazelden.

Thoreau, Henry David. 1961. *The Heart of Thoreau's Journals*. Edited by Odell Shepard. New York: Dover.

Thoreau, Henry David. 1983. *Walden and Civil Disobedience*. New York: Penguin.

Thoreau, Henry David. 2002. *Walking in the Essays of Henry Thoreau*. New York: North Point Press.

Tizard, Barbara, and Martin Hughes. 1984. *Children Learning at Home and in School*. London: Fontana Paperbacks.

Tolle, Eckhart. 2005. *The New Earth: Awakening to Life's Purpose*. New York: Dutton.

Turkle, Sherry. 2015. *Reclaiming Conversation: The Power of Talk in a Digital Age*. New York: Penguin.

Van Hook, Stephanie. 2015a. "Starting with Nonviolence." *Daily Metta* (7 September). Metta Center for Nonviolence. http://mettacenter.org/daily-metta/starting-with-nonviolence-daily-metta/.

Van Hook, Stephanie. 2015b. "Maria Montessori and Gandhiji." *Daily Metta* (31 August). Metta Center for Nonviolence. http://mettacenter.org/daily-metta/maria-montessori-and-gandhiji-daily-metta/.

Van Hook, Stephanie. 2015c. "Still Small Voice." *Daily Metta* (5 February). Metta Center for Nonviolence. http://mettacenter.org/daily-metta/still-small-voice-daily-metta/.

van Lommel, Pin. 2004. "About the Continuity of Our Consciousness." In *Brain Death and Disorders of Consciousness*, edited by Calixto Machado and D. Alan Shewmon, 115–32. New York: Springer. https://doi.org/10.1007/978-0-306-48526-8_9.

Watts, Alan. 1995. *The Tao of Philosophy: The Edited Transcripts*. Boston: Charles E. Tuttle.

West, Cornel. 2008. *Hope on a Tightrope: Words and Wisdom*. New York: Hay House.

Wilber, Ken, ed. 1984. *Quantum Questions*. Boston: Shambhala.

Wilson, Colin. 1985. *Rudolf Steiner: The Man and His Vision*. Wellingborough, UK: Aquarian Press.

Wintler, Justin. 2008. *Perfect Hostage: A Life of Aung San Suu Kyi, Burma's Prisoner of Conscience*. New York: Skyhorse Publishing.

Ywahoo, Dhyani. 1987. *Voices of Our Ancestors: Cherokee Teachings from the Wisdom Fire*. Boston: Shambhala.

Index

www.ingramcontent.com/pod-product-compliance
Lightning Source LLC
Chambersburg PA
CBHW030250030426
42336CB00009B/323